Indians of Burke County
and Western North Carolina

Larry Richard Clark

Award
Outstanding Writers of North Carolina History
North Carolina Society of Historians

TimeSpan Press

LIBRARY OF CONGRESS CATALOGUING-IN-PUBLICATION DATA

Clark, Larry Richard, 1940 -
Indians of Burke County and Western North Carolina/Larry Richard Clark

ISBN-10: 1453762086
ISBN-13: 978-1453762080
softcover : Times New Roman text

1. Southern States — American Indian. 2. North Carolina — South Carolina —
Tennessee. 3. Spain — Fort San Juan — Joara. 4. Prehistoric — 16th century.

First Edition 2002. Updated 2010.
Updated CreateSpace © 2016 Larry Richard Clark. All rights reserved.

Front Cover: Detail from mural painting by Greg Harlin courtesy of Frank H.
McClung Museum, The University of Tennessee at Knoxville. Illustrations:
Graphics and photographs by author unless otherwise credited.

TimeSpan Press
2880 Irish Creek Road
Morganton, NC 28655

PREFACE TO CURRENT EDITION

Indians of Burke County and Western North Carolina was first published in a spiral binder more than a decade ago as a limited edition to satisfy a local interest in "Indians," a subject encouraged by recent archaeological excavations within Burke County. Although the following, version is somewhat dated, this little book continues to provide the general reader a convenient overview of prehistoric Native Americans who once lived in the Appalachian foothills of western North Carolina and Burke County. Hopefully, this brief encounter with our Native American heritage will encourage you to read further. The bibliography offers a variety of references for additional study.

Decades earlier, surveys of the upper Catawba River by the Research Laboratories of Archaeology at UNC-Chapel Hill, U.S. Forest Service and State Historic Preservation Office had recorded hundreds of prehistoric and early historic sites for future study. In addition, David Moore of Warren Wilson College initiated "The Upper Catawba Valley Archaeology Project," an effort designed to study a 16th century native town on the Berry's farm in northern Burke County — but eventually uncovered evidence of Spaniards arriving to construct a fort and remain for eighteen months.

Since then, archaeologist David Moore, Robin Beck and others have concluded that Hernando de Soto arrived here from Tampa Bay in 1541 and then, two decades later, Captain Juan Pardo came to construct a *presidio* along Upper Creek in Burke County — the earliest European settlement in the interior of what is now the United States. Currently known as the native town of "Joara" and Spain's "Fort San Juan," this exciting discovery serves to increase our need to better understand the peoples who occupied this land for thousands of years prior to the arrival of Europeans and, furthermore, encourages the protection and preservation of this fragile Native American heritage for future generations.

Larry Richard Clark
Burke County, North Carolina

Conch shell gorget (necklace) found near the Catawba River
in Burke County. Original is approximately three inches in
diameter with a Late Woodland/Mississippian design
representing a coiled rattlesnake. Author's photograph.

WE ARE BROTHERS

*Together, side by side, my brothers we dance the Round Dance,
good and free. Cast away your fears and hate. No time left to
discriminate among ourselves. We are Brothers.*

*Apache, Seminole and Cherokee too, make room in this
Round Dance for a Sioux. Says he's half-breed, has no
white kin. Says he's Indian, let him in. We are Brothers.*

*Together, side by side, my brothers we dance the Round Dance,
good and free. We are Brothers.*

"Sea-Flower" from *Akwesasne Notes*,
volume 3, Number 8 (1971), 48.

TABLE OF CONTENTS

Other Publications by the Author

The Last Conquistadors of Southeast North America:
Pedro Menendez and the Collapse of La Florida's Frontier

La Florida: Imperial Spain Invades Indian Chiefdoms
of North America 1513-1543

Spanish Attempts to Colonize Southeast North America: 1513-1587

Burke County, North Carolina:
Historic Tales from the Gateway to the Blue Ridge

Time Capsules: the Why, the How, the Where

TAWODI (historical novel)
Cherokee of the Blue Mountains
Confront Spanish conquistadors

Brief Account of Prehistoric Times

Geology and Geography: Humans have lived in and around present day Burke County for approximately 12,000 years. While hard evidence of their earliest arrival into western North Carolina is lacking at this point, recent research throughout North America by geologists and archaeologists provide a plausible reconstruction of these ancient times and reasonable guesses as to the people who likely subsisted on this land. From this perspective, the initial questions needing an answer are: "Where did these first Native Americans originate?" "How and when did they arrive in North America?" "How and when did they settle in western North Carolina and Burke County?"

People lived in the Old World long before any decided to migrate into the Americas. It seems our earliest hominid ancestors, such as *Australopithecus afarensis*, originated in Africa almost four million years ago. A more advanced *Homo erectus* appeared ca. 250,000 years ago to begin the Paleolithic culture (Old Stone Age) and it would be their descendants, *Homo sapiens*, who migrated out of Africa to populate Europe and Asia about 100,000 years ago. As food collectors and hunters, these Paleolithic peoples successfully obtained the basic necessities for living: raised families, buried their dead, worshiped their gods and created diverse cultures in order to survive even the harshest environments. Their cunning behaviors and simple stone, bone and wood tools made them masters of their domain.

Migrating game animals, as well as changes in climate over eons, forced these earliest humans to periodically move into new and unexplored territories. One of the most dramatic climatic events to occur during the past two million years were a series of Ice Ages which resulted in colder temperatures around the world with massive ice flows from the north and south poles — and interglacial periods with warmer temperatures and melting ice. Four glacial periods, with each lasting thousands of years, produced at times an average world temperature decrease of twenty degrees Fahrenheit. As described by J. L. Stuckey in *North Carolina: Its Geology and Mineral Resources*, mountains of ice up to 3,000 feet thick slowly slipped into North America and along the Appalachian Mountains as ocean levels dropped by hundreds of feet to expose vast coastal plains. As each glacial epoch ended and tons of ice melted, mighty rivers roared across the earth and ancient oceans rose higher to flood these same coastal regions.

During the world's last major glaciation between 30,000-10,000 BP (Before Present), large regions of Europe, Siberia, Canada and the northern United States — as far south as the mid-Atlantic region — were covered in arctic snow and ice. This "Wisconsin Stage" had a profound effect upon the earth's flora and fauna which had to either adapt to a colder climate, move into new ecological niches or die-out completely. For example, scientific studies reveal arctic tundra and boreal forest in most mountain regions of North America during a high point in the

1

Wisconsin Stage. In addition, archaeological excavations find evidence of woolly mammoth in the west, mastodon in the east, caribou in Connecticut, musk oxen in Arkansas and walrus along the Virginia coast. Bear and deer, along with a now extinct horse and camel, were also common in North America before humans arrived.

The Appalachian Mountains (today greatly eroded by time and weather) were uplifted to great heights some 65 million years ago. During the last Ice Age of the Pleistocene epoch, arctic boreal forest migrated southward into the lower valleys and foothills of the Blue Ridge Mountains and some geologists even suggest parts of the Appalachian Mountains above 5,000 feet contained permanent snow fields and glacial ice (Michalek). Beginning about 10,000 BP with the present day Holocene interglacial epoch, warming trends forced most cooler climate flora and fauna species to retreat northward but left many species behind in the southern Appalachians as isolated populations which eventually acquired their own unique characteristics. As one of the oldest mountain ranges in the world, more species of trees and shrubs are present today in the southern Appalachian Mountains than in all of Europe. Its eastern slopes, especially, contain certain rare temperate flora found no where else in the world — along with typical northern habitat trees and shrubs. Recent research of animal populations in the Great Smoky Mountains also reveal a rich fauna diversity not known before.

In the *Global Atlas of Paleovegetation* Adams and Faure describe most of the hills and mountains east of the Mississippi River at 18,000 BP as "closed boreal-type pine" (*Pinus*) and conifer (*Picea*) woodlands where broadleaf deciduous trees such as the oak, maple, popular and sycamore were less abundant than at present. Pollen core samples and radiocarbon dates indicate the Appalachian Mountains contained patches of permafrost at evaluations above 2,500 feet. With a drier climate along the Atlantic coast, Jack Pine appeared as the dominant tree with desert-type xerophytic plants on sandy dunes which stretched inland into the Piedmont region. Not until thousands of years later did the eastern woodlands of North America become dominated by oak trees which now comprise about forty percent of its mixed deciduous forest.

These Ice Ages not only reshaped the earth but greatly influenced the destiny of human populations around the globe by encouraging migrations on a grand scale across Africa, Europe, Asia and, eventually, as far as Australia. A significant impact on North America occurred as Alaska and Siberia became connected by ice and a land bridge due to lower ocean levels. Thereafter, around 12,000 BP, Siberian Paleolithic hunters began to follow game animals eastward into Alaska and Canada where no humans lived. There is also increasing evidence that shifts in Pacific Ocean currents could have created a milder coastal climate along the Bering Straits for these ancient travelers.

In recent years, Ross MacPhee of the American Museum of Natural History introduced a new factor into this complex view of climatic and ecological change — the arrival of lethal germs into North America. MacPhee hypothesizes that these same forces dramatically affected flora and fauna adaptation during the Wisconsin Stage also influenced the smallest organisms, bacteria and viruses. The arrival of humans into North America, along with their dogs and any hitchhiking pests, could have introduced deadly diseases among New World mammals such as the giant ground sloth, camel, horse and bear-sized beaver. This event alone could explain a mystery surrounding the rapid disappearance of these animals, which many current text books continue to attribute solely to overkill from hunting by the newly arrived human immigrants.

The Siberian route was first suggested by Jose de Acosta, a Jesuit missionary living in South America during the 16th century, as a theory for the origin of the first peoples in North America. His idea remained dominant into the 20th century and resulted in an assumption that these Paleolithic hunters could not have reached the Atlantic coast and southern tip of South America until thousands of years later. However, more recently research considers the distinct possibility that the first humans to arrive in South America could have arrived from the oceans several thousand years earlier.

In a past issue of *Scientific American*, Sasha Nemecek identified several ancient peoples of the Pacific and Asia who possessed the ability to construct simple boats and, either by accident or by design, landed on the Pacific shores of the Americas at least 15,000 years ago. In addition, other researchers suggest a south Atlantic boat route for east coast sea travelers from Europe and Africa. It also appears that an ice and land bridge existed in the north Atlantic between the British Isles, Greenland and Canada. This could allow a westward passage to northern European Neolithic (New Stone Age) peoples. Recent blood research studies in several Eskimo communities in Canada have identified two specific DNA traits most often found among European populations.

Wikimedia Commons "Storyteller." Courtesy artist Howard Terpning.

Wisconsin Glaciation Maximum ca. 18,000 BP

The Wisconsin glaciation radically altered the geography of North America north of the Ohio River. Today, during the Holocene epoch, the arctic ice sheets continue to retreat and are greatly reduced during summer months. Image above adapted from McDaniel College department of paleoecology graphics found on the Web.

The First Americans: When attempting to study the thousands of years people have inhabited North America, scholars are presented with a bewildering array of conjecture and evidence. Without the benefit of written records, they must turn to the camp sites, simple tools and buried remains of ancient humans to answer the questions: "What do prehistoric artifacts tell us about the people who once lived there?" "When did they arrive and how long did they occupy an area?" "What contacts were made with other groups and how did their cultures change over time?"

Based upon current knowledge, archaeologist have devised a chronology of cultural periods for many regions of North America to aid in telling this exciting story. For example, wandering Paleolithic hunters were the first arrivals into an area, followed thousands of years later by Archaic settlers and then, much later, by Woodland farmers. This simplified view of *prehistoric* Native Americans ends as they, and their cultures, are overtaken by the arrival of "civilized" Europeans during the 16th century — who write them into history.

Siberia was populated with several Paleolithic human populations before 35,000 BP and it will be these "Asians" who migrate into North America over the Bering Straits land-ice corridor. Those who moved southward into the Americas will become known as Indians while those settling in northern Canada became Eskimos. The term "Eskimo" is thought to be derived from a New England Ojibway word, *Askkimey*, meaning "people of the north who eat raw meat." The term "Indian" was provided by Christopher Columbus to describe the natives found in the Caribbean islands because he mistakenly thought his ships had arrived on the coast of India — thus, these people must be "*Indios.*"

Archaeological and paleontological evidence confirm these small, extended family groups of Paleolithic hunters were living in the American Southwest by 13,500 BP. In addition to hunting large animals, they collected plant foods and trapped small game to provide a varied diet. This early prehistoric Indian culture is identified as "Clovis" after an archaeological site excavated near Clovis, New Mexico, which provided enough materials to characterize these ancient people. Another, more complex Clovis site was later found at Blackwater Draw, New Mexico. Today prehistoric Clovis-like Native American sites have been found throughout much of the United States.

The primary diagnostic artifact of the Clovis people is the fluted spear point, a narrow, thin, leaf-shaped stone point 2-4 inches long with a fluted (chipped) channel on both sides of its base. (See following illustrations.) Folsom and Plano are two other cultural types associated with later Paleo-Indians where fluted points, scrapers, knives and other stone tools are found at kill sites with the remains of now extinct bison, mammoth, horse and camel. Evidently these hunters captured huge feast by stampeding animals over cliffs or trapping them in a gully. Folsom and Plano artifacts always appear above excavated Clovis materials and, therefore, are considered to be more recent in time. The Clovis-Folsom-Plano cultural sequence dates the Paleo-Indian period in southwest North America between 13,500 - 10,000 BP.

Characteristic Paleo-Indian Spear Points

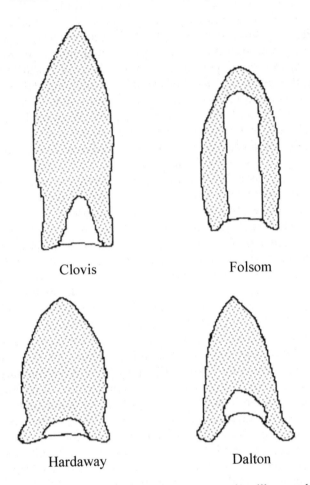

Clovis   Folsom

Hardaway   Dalton

Note the "flutes" (light areas) in the spear points illustrated above. These flakes are chipped from both sides to allow the point to fit into a split wood spear shaft. The associated "lamellae flakes," are used as blades for cutting. Lamellae flakes are significant finds during surface collecting and excavations. Hardaway, the oldest confirmed Paleo-Indian point in North Carolina, (ca. 12,000 B.P.) is found in various sizes across the state.

At this juncture we should pose another interesting question: "Are the Clovis-Folsom-Plano peoples the earliest Native Americans in the United States?" Since our knowledge of the past is always changing, we must keep an open mind to the possibility that new evidence may appear tomorrow which dramatically alters our concept and understanding of prehistoric Native Americans. For example, in contradiction to the Siberian-Bering Strait passage, several sites in eastern North America suggest the first Native Americans may have arrived along the east coast and then moved inland. Cactus Hill and the Notoway River Site in Virginia have produced evidence of a pre-Clovis occupation. The Topper Site, along the Savannah River in South Carolina, was identified as a Clovis site for many years; however, when Al Goodyear returned to excavate deeper he discovered additional, unrelated artifacts below the previous Clovis culture level. Meadowcroft Rockshelter in Pennsylvania has consistently produced radiocarbon dates of 13,000 BP from the remains of prehistoric baskets and animal snares — which supports James Adovasio's claim that women, children and the elderly devoted a major effort to plant gathering and small game. In North Carolina the Hardaway site, excavated by Joffre Coe and dated at about 12,000 BP, has produced Clovis-like spear points.

The most exciting dates for the Paleolithic Period, however, are suggested for South America by Tom Dillehay and others at the Monte Verde site in Chile. With radiocarbon dates of 14,500 BP Monte Verde becomes the oldest known location of human habitation anywhere in the Americas. This campsite produced the remains of tents, wooden tools, animal hides, a human footprint and evidence that ocean fishing may have been central to their lifestyle. Other and similar ancient sites have been located in Argentina, Peru and Colombia. A female skull dated at 13,500 BP has been uncovered in Brazil, the oldest date so far for human skeletal remains in either North or South America (not to overlook the recent discovery in Oregon, USA, of fossilized human feces dated at 14,000 BP.) More recently, the skeletal remains of a teenage female was found in an underwater cave in Mexico, with DNA intact, which is dated near 13,000 BP.

These earlier dates spread across the Americas raise serious questions about Clovis being the oldest Paleolithic culture and the Siberian-Bering Straits offers the only path for Paleolithic travelers. Therefore, future research must be directed toward the possibility that boats from Asia and Africa brought some of the first humans to the New World while others traveled by foot along an ice-land corridor from Europe to Canada.

Eastern U. S. Major Geo-Cultural Areas
(After Kroeber, *Cultural and Natural Areas of America.*)

The North Carolina geo-cultural area includes the Appalachian Mountains, a region from northern Georgia into eastern Pennsylvania with the Southern Appalachian Summit including North Carolina, Georgia and Tennessee. Another geographic area includes the east and west foothills of the Appalachian Mountains — which for North Carolina reach into the Piedmont. Thousands of years ago a larger Coastal Plains stretched from New England to the Gulf of Mexico.

HOW THE WORLD WAS MADE
(Adapted from James Mooney, *Myths of the Cherokees*.)

The world is a great island floating within a great cavern on a sea of water, suspended at four corners by cords hanging from the sky. When the world grows to old, these cords will break and the earth will sink into the ocean and all the people will die. Before the world was made, all was water and the animals lived above in the sky and wanted more room. They wondered what was beneath the water and sent Water-Beetle to find out. He darted in all directions over the water but found no where to rest. He dived deep below the surface and came up with mud, which began to grow in all directions. This became Earth. Later Earth was tied with four cords, but no one remembers who did this.

The animals sent birds below to see if they could live there, but the land was very wet and soft. Finally, they sent the Great Buzzard to investigate but the land was still wet. When he became to tired to fly, he landed and flapped his wings to cool off. Everywhere his wing tips struck the earth there was a valley and when he raised his wings there was a mountain. This was to be the Cherokee country.

When the earth was dry the animals came down, but it was dark. They took the sun and set it to cross the island and under the sea each day -- but this was to hot and Tsiska'gili, the Red Crayfish, scorched his shell bright red. This spoiled his meat and, therefore, he is not eaten even today. The conjurers kept pushing the sun higher and higher until it finally reached seven hands high, the highest place of all they now call Gulkwa'gine Di'galun'altiyun, "the seventh height."

There is another world beneath the surface which is like ours in every way with animals, plants and people, but the seasons are different. It is warmer in winter and cooler in summer. We reach the underworld by following mountain streams to their source into the earth. These are the doorways we may enter after fasting, bathing and finding one of the underground people to lead us.

When animals and plants were first made, they were told to be awake and watch for seven nights, just as young men now fast and pray seven nights to earn their power. Only the owl, panther and one or two more could stay awake. These animals were given the power to travel at night in the dark and feed on those who sleep. Among plants, only the cedar, pine, spruce, holly and laurel were awake to receive the power to always be green and to provide the best medicine.

People came after plants and animals. At first there was only a sister and a brother until he struck her with a fish and told her to multiply. And so it was. In seven days a child was born to her, and thereafter every seven days another until the world had to many people. Then it was made that a woman should have only one child in a year.

All was in harmony among plants, animals and people until the people again increased in number so much that they took to many animals for food. So the animals devised many sicknesses to control the people. The bond between animals and people was broken. Only the plants remained a friend of people and provided cures for sickness.

Key Terms and Dates

Archaic Period 8000-1000 BC is referred to as a "Forest Efficiency Culture" during this time in North Carolina. These nomadic Native Americans lived in hunting camps and, eventually, small seasonal villages along waterways. Used the atlatl, a short throwing spear.

Artifacts are material objects which indicate human adaptation or construction. Prehistoric sites most often reveal artifacts of clay or stone, since wood and bone normally decay in a relatively brief period of time.

Culture is the lifestyle of a particular people, including their manufactured products and utilized resources which reflect their behaviors. Archaeologist reconstruct a past culture from specific artifacts (e.g. tools, pottery and weapons) and associated evidence found in huts, postholes, burials and soil samples.

Cultural Context: An artifact found in soil below another level is considered older. Those objects found at the same level, horizontally, are typically thought to be of the same age and the same culture; therefore, all of these items are related one to another within this particular cultural context and time period.

Dendrochronology is the scientific measurement of tree rings. Where preserved ancient logs are found, archaeologists match the growth rings through several soil levels with trees at the surface to determine an approximate age for a site.

Flora and Fauna Analysis: Preserved nuts, seeds, pollen and animal bones carefully collected during excavation provide important information about a people's lifestyle. Radiocarbon dates may be determined from organic remains. Soil samples examined under a microscope may reveal pollen spores which allows the identification of tree and plant species.

Historic Period after 1540: When Spanish *conquistadors* arrived in western North Carolina, written histories of those native tribes began. The English arrived decades later on the Atlantic coast at Roanoke Island (Sir Walter Raleigh's "Lost Colony"). France began to travel down the Mississippi River from Canada. These contacts forever changed the destiny of Native Americans.

Holocene Epoch 10,000 BP - Present: This is the earth's current geological period which began with the end of the Pleistocene Epoch and the last major ice age known in North America as the Wisconsin Ice Age.

Mississippian Phase 1300 - 1700 AD: As a more complex Late Woodland culture evolved, certain tribes in the southeast constructed ceremonial earthen mounds and large, walled towns, adopted corn agriculture and developed highly decorative pottery and elaborate ceremonial customs.

Paleolithic: The oldest human cultures are identified as "Old Stone Age" or Paleolithic cultures dated at about 150,000 years BP in Europe and about 15,000 BP in the New World. For North Carolina, one must remember that near arctic climates existed in the western mountains and foothills when coastal sea levels were more than 100 feet lower than today.

Pleistocene Epoch 2 million - 10,000 BP is a geological period when several major and minor ice ages occurred on earth. Arctic and near arctic weather was evident over much of earth's northern hemisphere.

Prehistoric is a period of time in a particular location before the appearance of written records and human civilizations. "Protohistoric" cultures occur immediately before their transition into a literate, civilized people.

Projectile Point describes an artifact most often constructed of stone, bone or wood attached to a stick and used as a spear or an arrow. The smallest "bird points" were used with blowgun darts.

Radiocarbon Date: All living things absorb two different isotopes of carbon, C12 and C14. At death, carbon 14 decays at a predictable rate. Once an ancient sample of bone or wood is processed, a date is calculated. Radiocarbon dates are often written to show a margin of error, e.g. BC 970 ± 110 years.

Sequence Dating requires an adequate number of artifacts of a particular type (e.g., pottery) where further study finds similarities and differences in design, manufacture and/or materials over time. Plotting these characteristics on a chart may reveal that type A (lowest level) matches type B and others found at upper cultural levels. This sequence provides relative dates for this particular artifact and may date other artifacts found in association at each level.

Site is a geographic location which exhibits evidence of human occupation by a prehistoric or historic people. Once discovered, an archaeological excavation may occur after an intensive surface survey and the excavation of test pits.

Stratigraphy: Over long periods of time water, wind, heat and cold produce characteristic earth sediments and soils layered one upon the other. At a site these stratified layers of soil represent periods of time where the surface is most recent and each distinctive lower level becomes progressively older.

Temper: Native Americans mixed a variety of local materials into their pottery clays to improve its properties. The temper materials most often added to clay included sand, grass, crushed rock or shells.

Typology: Artifacts are first sorted by their general characteristics, e.g. points, knives, axes, hammer stones, etc. Laboratory analysis sorts each item into additional categories based upon (1) differences in manufacturing techniques, (2) materials used and (3) comparisons to all other known types in a category. Eventually, an artifact may be described as a Clovis-type chert spear point.

Woodland Period 1000 BC - 1700 AD: A time when some, but not all, North Carolina tribes became farmers, typically living along river bottomland to grow corn, beans, squash and pumpkin. In some regions they built fortified towns and organized as large chiefdoms that included dozens of villages. Well made clay pottery is introduced along with the bow and arrow.

An Overview of North Carolina Prehistory

Paleolithic Period: The first humans most likely arrived in the coastal region of North Carolina at some point during the last half of the Wisconsin glacial period, most likely before 12,000 BP. In succeeding centuries, as winters gradually became milder and summers longer, the state's western hills and mountains transformed from boreal woodlands into hardwood forest of oak, maple, popular and birch. Arctic fauna were replaced with the deer, elk, bison, rabbit, squirrel and even smaller creatures of the forest as temperate plants with their eatable berries, nuts and roots became abundant along fast flowing rivers and streams.

As elsewhere across North America, North Carolina's Paleo-Indians lived as small, nomadic extended families that constantly moved with the seasons in search of needed resources. As hunters and foragers, these ancient people adapted to local environments and created a sophisticated assortment of tools and habits to survive. They carried their processions from one location to another and built no permanent dwellings. Protection from severe weather consisted of small huts constructed from sticks and brush, forest thickets or the occasional rock shelter. Clothes and floor mats were made from plant fibers and animal hides. Containers most likely included bark and animal bags, gourds and woven nets from vines or grass. Today, only their camp fires and stone implements offer tantalizing clues for Paleo-Indians once living across this state where fewer than 100 Clovis-like fluted points have been found.

The Hardaway and Dalton fluted spear points, first identified in the Piedmont by Joffre Coe, are included among the oldest prehistoric artifacts in North Carolina. First found by an amateur archaeologists, the Hardaway site along the Yadkin River near Badin Lake in Stanley County is currently the oldest documented Paleolithic occupation in North Carolina. "Three sites have been examined and reported in detail," Coe writes for the American Philosophical Society, "and approximately 65,851 specimens were recovered, catalogued, and analyzed." From this evidence Coe concluded that the Carolina Piedmont experienced a definable cultural sequence from Paleo-Indian to Archaic, Woodland and historic. Hardaway points (1 - 2.5 inches) appear to be indigenous while the Dalton (2 - 3 inches) exhibits characteristics similar to those found further to the south. The Hardaway-Dalton cultural sequence generally dates the Paleo-Indian in North Carolina between 12,000-10,000 BP.

The Coastal Plains present several unique problems for Paleolithic research as the Wisconsin Ice Age ended and sea levels rose dramatically, flooding vast coastal areas and creating new marshlands. Many potential Paleo-Indian sites along the Carolina coast are thought to now lie beneath the Atlantic Ocean along the Continental Shelf (Phelps). Another significant difference, when compared to the piedmont and mountains, is that coastal Paleo-Indian cultures depended a great deal on sea foods, shells and wetland plants which are less likely to be preserved over thousands of years.

The mountains and foothills of western North Carolina have produced widely scattered Paleo-Indian artifacts of the Clovis-Hardaway-Dalton types but no significant undisturbed locations for this period exist at present. Part of the problem arises from the fact that these first mountaineers favored hill tops for their camps, thereby allowing centuries of rain and weather to erode these sites. This lack of Paleolithic evidence may also be due to smaller populations traveling in the rugged mountains of North Carolina — or due to less archaeological research activity in this region. However, most of the discovered mountain Paleo-Indian fluted points are produced from local stone which leads some to conclude that these ancient spear points were manufactured by resident Native Americans and not simply lost by seasonal hunting parties from outside the region. (Purrington 1983).

HOW WE OBTAINED FIRE

They say long ago there was no fire and the People ate their food uncooked. Then there were only two men who had fire, the People could see it in the tops of a very tall pine tree. Coyote proposed they come together for a dance. He suggested a message be sent to those who had fire -- asking them to bring some -- the People wanted to gamble with the Guessing Game.

At the dance, Coyote told his friends to tie dry grass around his tail. When it was daybreak, Coyote danced by himself and danced across the fire. "Your tail is on fire!" the men yelled to him. "Why do you say my tail is burning?" Coyote asked. They called to him again, "Your tail is burning!" Coyote danced around the fire four times and then jumped over the men and ran away with the fire. Those who owned the fire ran after him and put out the fire they found.

After they caught Coyote, the men stretched his nose so it is long and spread his mouth so that it is wide. Then Night Hawk ran away with the fire. They caught him after a long chase, pushed the crown of his head down and spread his mouth. Then another person ran with the fire. This was Turkey Buzzard. They caught him after a long race and pulled the feathers out of his head, but Buzzard had given the fire to Humming Bird.

Now the People looked at a high mountain in the distance. Fire was coming out the top. The People now came to have plenty of fire because of Coyote and the others. The fire went inside trees and became plentiful. (Western Apache. Adapted from Gloria Levitas et al, *American Indian Prose and Poetry*, 80-81.)

Archaic Period: Following thousands of years of Paleo-Indian culture, the Archaic Period (8000-1000 BC) arrives when Native Americans adapt to the increasingly wetter, warmer environment of the Holocene and the expanding hardwood forests of eastern North America. Often referred to as a Primary Forest Efficiency Culture, innovations create a wide assortment of stone, bone and wood implements which allows these people to successfully settle among North Carolina's coastal plains, piedmont waterways and mountain forest. While Archaic artifacts are similar across North Carolina, there is significant diversity in the tools and materials found at different sites, which explains, in part, why archaeologists typically divide this cultural period into lower, middle and upper Archaic.

Hunting deer and other game animals in dense forest and thick undergrowth improved with the appearance of a short spear and spear thrower. This hand-held throwing stick (*atlatl*), butted at the base to a smaller spear, provided improved leverage for a faster and more powerful throw. (See following illustration.) In addition, the older traditions of hunting, fishing and trapping were increasingly supplemented with intensive foraging for plant foods that included nuts, berries, roots and wild seed plants. The bearing trees of hickory, oak and chestnut spreading across North Carolina during the Holocene provided both Indians and forest game animals an abundant food source.

Archaeological evidence indicates camp sites were often revisited by different groups for centuries as native populations increased beyond the small, self-sufficient family bands of earlier millennia. Living in seasonal camps provided habitation and work areas as its members hunted and foraged for food over a large area. Dwellings were temporary structures of poles, tree limbs and branches covered with hides or woven mats. Although Early Archaic peoples continued to be organized as members of extended families, they probably had "clan leaders" cooperating among different family groups for the good of the larger community. Not until the Late Archaic do larger villages suggest the beginnings of tribal organization among several communities over a larger area.

Archaic Coastal Plains sites indicate sophisticated adaptations to wetland environments and inland waterways along with a gradual increase in population. Kirk and Stanly spear points are common. Later Archaic sites indicate a relatively homogeneous cultural assemblage often related to Savannah River cultures in the southeast and, also, the northeast Susquehanna River traditions (Phelps). Common coastal artifacts during this period include steatite (soapstone) vessels, decorative art and complex burials. Around 2000 BC the earliest pottery appears in North Carolina made of fiber tempered clay which most likely served as storage vessels for foods taken from inland waterways and ocean, hand-harvested and garden produce. Coastal Indians, like most other native groups during the Archaic, also engaged in long-distance trade. Archaeologists have found conch shells from the Gulf of Mexico carved into cups, spoons and pendants decorated with copper from the Great Lakes region.

Handheld Archaic Atlatl Spear Thrower.

Note the counterweight "bannerstone" attached to the end of a throwing stick. The long, slender Guilford spear point is associated with this shorter spear. A student of mine constructed an atlatl and, with practice, was able to strike a bale of hay at 100 yards.

In the Carolina Piedmont, many high hills reveal Archaic hunting camps and seasonal occupations are often larger and more complex than either coastal or mountain sites. Based upon excavations and research by Coe in the 1930s, the Piedmont projectile point types known as Kirk, Stanly, Morrow Mountain, Guilford and Savannah River have been the measure for other Archaic artifacts uncovered across North Carolina. Of some special interest, Piedmont Native Americans often traveled to Morrow Mountain, near Albemarle, to gather its fine-grained rhyolite stone for the manufacture of points and tools.

During the Late Archaic, Indians of the Carolina Piedmont adopted a more sedentary lifestyle with sites exhibiting burials, garbage pits and clay hearths. Although "slash-and-burn" gardening of a few select plants (slash tree bark to kill the trees and burn the undergrowth) may have occurred at this time, their year-round dietary favorites continued to be nuts, mollusk, fish, birds and the white-tail deer. (Ward 1983) Such foods would be boiled, fried, steamed or roasted into tasty concoctions and flavored with seeds, roots, honey, fruits or plant leaves. (See recipes in later section.) It is interesting to contemplate what forgotten Indian delicacies will never be found in excavation records, such as the corn parasite *ustilago maydis* (black corn smut) which turns field corn into puffy mushroom-like fungus balls. This aromatic, vitamin C rich substance continues to be used today in Central America as a flavoring for various native dishes.

Archaic cultural innovations appear somewhat later in western North Carolina, with particular influences from Tennessee and Georgia. These mountain sites are never quite as large or complex as those found in the Piedmont or Coastal Plains. From the Great Smoky Mountains northward into Watauga County, natives continued their hunting-foraging culture with a wide range of habitats from rock shelters and bald mountains to river floodplains. Morrow Mountain, Guilford and Savannah River assemblages are common throughout the region in the Middle and Late Archaic. (Purrington 1983) Unlike other areas of North Carolina, abundant supplies of crystal quartz, milky quartz and granular quartzite are the preferred materials for projectile points. Fine grained chert and jasper stone, as trade items from the west, are also found occasionally as points and tools. Local steatite, or "soapstone," appears to be a major trade item from North Carolina, since it is found at Native American sites in the southeast and midwest where no local deposits exist. The Blue Rock Quarry in Yancey County contains a large 10 foot tall outcrop of soapstone (an impure form of talcy rock) pockmarked with evidence of native "mining" over many centuries.

Typical Archaic Stone Tools and Hearth-ware
[NOT TO SCALE]

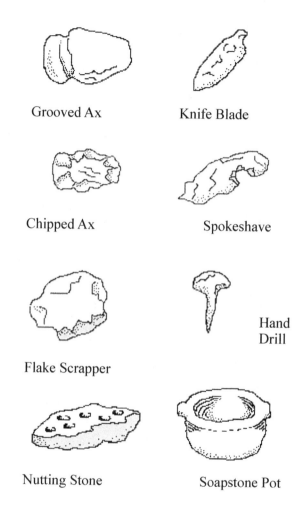

Grooved Ax

Knife Blade

Chipped Ax

Spokeshave

Flake Scrapper

Hand Drill

Nutting Stone

Soapstone Pot

The ax heads and a knife blade above were attached to wooden handles. The spokeshave is a small, slotted tool used to smooth and shave bark from spear shafts. Scrappers are often sharp stone flakes used to remove skin from hides. Flakes were also used as a cutting blade. The hand drill can produce holes in clay or bone. Sharpened deer antlers were used as an awl to punch holes in animal hides. Nutting stones held nuts in place while cracked with a rock. Steatite pots were shaped by ax and blade from a soapstone boulder, bottom-side up on a pedestal and then broken-off to carve out the inside.

Early Archaic Spear Points 8000 - 5000 BC

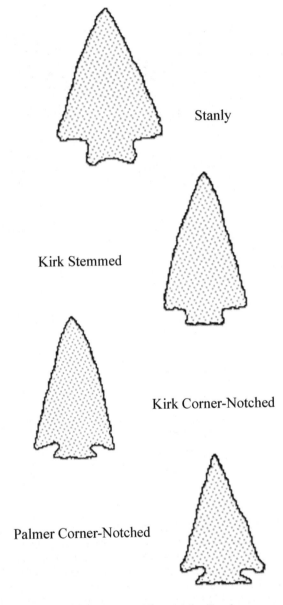

Stanly

Kirk Stemmed

Kirk Corner-Notched

Palmer Corner-Notched

From bottom to top, the Palmer is older and the Stanly more recent.
After Joffre L. Coe, *The Formative Cultures of the Carolina Piedmont.*

Late Archaic Spear Points 5000 - 1000 BC

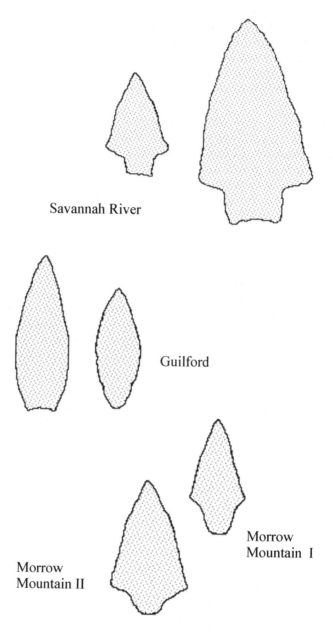

Savannah River

Guilford

Morrow
Mountain I

Morrow
Mountain II

From bottom to top the Morrow Mountain is older and the
Savannah River more recent. After Joffre L. Coe, *The
Formative Cultures of the Carolina Piedmont.*

Woodland Period: Archaeologists know a great deal more about the Woodland Period (1000 BC-1000 AD) than earlier prehistoric times as numerous, easily accessible sites are found across North Carolina. In addition these cultural assemblages are much larger and more varied than the Archaic or Paleolithic. Being more recent also increases the odds for recovering associated flora and fauna materials. Stephen Claggett in "North Carolina's First Colonists" concludes that intensive gardening created this dramatic cultural transformation with evidence often found at Woodland sites. It is this knowledge of horticulture which encouraged Native Americans to adopt corn, beans, squash and pumpkin as common garden crops.

Many Early Woodland communities also engaged in extensive trade, constructed permanent towns and added the bow and arrow to their hunting gear. Well constructed houses were square, rectangle or round with thatched roofs and vertical walls sticks and mud. Woodland economies flourished as skillful artisans created decorative and functional pottery, jewelry, tools and clothing. Along with a growing population, certain Woodland towns also created more complex social systems with tribes, chiefdoms and priest. In addition, as mountain and Piedmont communities became truly forest efficient cultures, Native Americans along the Atlantic coast adapted their lifestyle to marshlands, estuaries and tidewater environments with the use of flat bottom boats, shallow water traps, spear fishing and nets with stone sinkers.

Where projectile points are important in differentiating between Paleo-Indian and Archaic cultures, pottery is the primary artifact used to characterize different Woodland cultures. Although Native Americans failed to discover the potter's wheel (an Old World invention), they did manufacture useful ceramic vessels for cooking, food storage and human burial by hand coiling and smoothing clay into various shapes and sizes. It is during the Woodland Period that North Carolina's crude, red clay ceramics evolved into fine-crafted pottery with innovative styles and elaborate, inscribed decorations. This durable artifact, with its variations in temper and designs, permits archaeologist to date pottery sequences for many of the ceramic traditions found across the state.

Human graves are another important way for archaeologists to date a site (radiocarbon) and to extrapolate on the meaning of a people's social structure and beliefs about an afterlife. Woodland Indians buried their dead with respect and ceremony, using a variety of customs that included single graves, cremations, mass graves, and disconnected human bones interned in clay pots or cloth bundles. On occasion excavated burials include weapons and personal items such as tool kits and decorative ornaments which reveal much about an individual and a tribe's ceremonial practices. Archaeologist David Phelps found numerous burials in North Carolina's coastal regions where cremation was the preferred burial custom; however, flexed and re-deposited articulated skeletons are common among the Waccamaw along the southern coast while Late Woodland Algonkin to the north favored mass interments similar to an Iroquoian tradition.

Although Tidewater natives subsisted primarily on shellfish and continued to occupy seasonal camps, the Tuscarora further inland appear to be planting corn by the Late Woodland and living in relatively large villages. Polished axes (celts), shell hoes, shell gorgets, bone awls, grass mats and columella beads are associated artifacts and, like other tribes of that time, the Tuscarora changed their hunting technology to the bow with arrows tipped with the Gypsy and Roanoke triangular point. While earlier coastal pottery was most often tempered with sand and made into thick, red clay vessels with pointed bases, their clays were now mixed with moss, dried grass, crushed shell or sand to improve its handling properties and constructed with flat bottoms to be decorated with carved paddles or fabric impressed designs. (Phelps)

In the Carolina Piedmont, most sites are located near rivers and, on occasion, found with large heaps of mussel shells (shell middens) after consuming this readily available food. Considered by archaeologists to be a significant excavation feature, these prehistoric garbage dumps may also include discarded household items along with the bones of game animals such as deer, raccoon, turkey, groundhog and bear. Characteristic Piedmont Woodland arrow points include the Yadkin, Pee Dee and Roanoke. (See following illustrations.) While hunting and foraging continued to provide food resources, an increase in horticulture along river bottomlands saw the appearance of corn as a major food crop by 1000 AD. Large, conical ceramic pots characteristic of food storage vessels are present at this time with cord or fabric impressed designs.

Several northern piedmont sites along the Dan River appear to be most closely associated with Virginia native cultures. As described by Trawick Ward (1983), Saura Town sand tempered pottery is most often decorated with net impressed, curvilinear complicated stamped and corn cob impressed designs and a small, triangular arrow point appears to be affiliated with areas further north. Many storage and refuse pits dot this large Woodland town with houses constructed as circular, dome-roofed structures up to thirty feet in diameter with mud ("wattle and daub") walls. Another particularly interesting feature at Saura Town includes "earthen ovens" and clay lined pits constructed for cooking fires.

The mountains and foothills of western North Carolina would eventually adopt many Woodland cultural traditions — but with several differences. First, these original mountaineers were relatively late in developing horticulture and larger villages. While other parts of North Carolina experienced significant population growth along lowland plains, Burton Purrington (1983) concludes that Indians of the Appalachian Summit essentially continued their small group Archaic traditions for an additional several centuries. Even with the introduction of pottery by 500 BC there appears a "wide range of mountain habitats with no noticeable increase in utilization of river bottoms," which is associated with the sedentary life-style of the Woodland farmer. If eventually confirmed, these developments will produce a Woodland prehistory for the North Carolina mountains somewhat different from the Piedmont and Coastal Plains. (See Keel, Bass, Dickens)

Typical Woodland Artifacts 1000 BC - 1000 AD
[NOT TO SCALE]

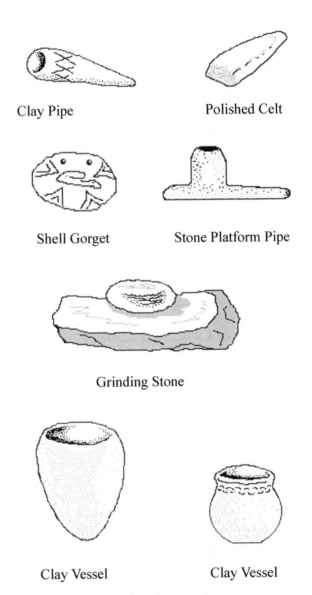

Clay Pipe

Polished Celt

Shell Gorget

Stone Platform Pipe

Grinding Stone

Clay Vessel

Clay Vessel

Pipes and tobacco were most likely used during religious and social ceremonies. A polished celt, attached to a stick, was used as an ax. Large shells or flat stones could also be utilized as hoes. Shell gorgets are decorative items worn around the neck. Dried corn, acorns, chestnuts and seeds were ground for cooking.. Clay pots for cooking and storage.

Only the Great Smoky Mountains and similar southern Appalachian Summit areas indicate Woodland Native Americans moved into these valleys with intensive agriculture and substantial trade with outside tribes. One such site was found in Jackson County where archaeologist David Moore conducted salvage excavations with the help of more than 100 volunteers. This work revealed three distinct features which included an earth lodge, burials and a fortified town. Similar sites are located in Macon County along Coweeta Creek and the upper Little Tennessee River. (See Keel and Egloff 1999, Rodning) In northwestern North Carolina, Purrington finds that Middle and Late Woodland changes from Pigeon check-stamped ceramics to a less impressive Connestee pottery which begs the question: "Was this indicative of a local indigenous pottery tradition without significant contact with the south?" He further offers a series of additional questions that must be answered to ultimately understand the mountain Indian cultures during the Late Woodland. For example, why does there appear to be a greater degree of Ohio Hopewellian influence in the southern Appalachian Summit than in the north (Chapman and Keel) and how much impact did north Georgia and east Tennessee native cultures have upon western North Carolina?

ORIGIN OF WHITE CORN

An old woman lived with her grandson. She made good sofki for the boy and it tasted good to him. The boy wanted to know where his grandmother got the white corn to make sofki, so the next time he sneaked back to watch her. She went into her hut and sat down. Her ankles were sore, very dry with flakes of skin. The boy watched as she scraped off these flakes and took them into the hut. The grandmother put the flakes into a pot with water. "That's were the sofki comes from," he thought.

After that day the boy would not drink sofki. His grandmother said, "Why do you not drink sofki?" The boy could not answer. Suspecting the boy had seen her, she told him that the people must now burn down their house with everything inside -- including the grandmother who did not want to live. A few days after it burned, the people and boy returned to find the house restored and full of corn. From that place the corn spread over all the earth. (Seminole. Adapted from Gloria Levitas et al, *American Indian Prose and Poetry*, 11.)

Late Woodland Town

An engraving by German printer Theodore de Bry taken froma a watercolor painting by English artist John White who traveled in 1585 to Roanoke Island, North Carolina. His inscription stated: *"The towne of Pomeiock and true forme of their howses, couered and enclosed some wth matts, and some wth barcks of trees. All compassed abowt wth smale poles stock thick together in stedd of a wall."* Courtesy of American Memory Online, Rare Book and Special Collections Division, Library of Congress.

Representative Woodland Arrow Points

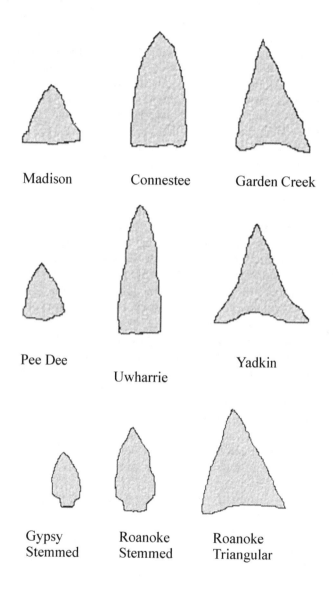

Madison   Connestee   Garden Creek

Pee Dee   Yadkin

Uwharrie

Gypsy   Roanoke   Roanoke
Stemmed   Stemmed   Triangular

Mississippian Phase: Scholars have determined that after 1000 AD certain tribes along the upper Mississippi River and its tributaries experienced cultural, economic and social changes which significantly affected their Late Woodland lifestyles. Referred to as the "Mississippian Phase" these innovations did not occur equally among all native groups, although some elements of Mississippian culture did spread southward to the Gulf of Mexico and into Georgia, South Carolina and North Carolina. The more significant characteristics of Mississippian culture include intensive corn agriculture supplemented with hunting and foraging, a distinctive pottery style, complex social systems and, especially, ceremonial earthen mounds. L. C. Rampton in *The Native Americans* described this phase as a "Temple Mound Tradition." (Spencer and Jennings) As a late prehistoric or protohistoric event, it is these earthen burial and ceremonial mounds that are most distinctive. During its peak, Mississippian chiefs and religious leaders governed from large, spectacular ceremonial towns, places today known as Fort Ancient (Ohio), Kincaid (Illinois), Etowah (Georgia), Moundville (Alabama), Spiro (Oklahoma) and Cahokia (Missouri) where one mound rises some 100 feet high and covers sixteen acres. It is this region which appears to be the geographic center for these "mound builders" and for the most advanced North American native societies of prehistoric times.

While North Carolina tribes used their considerable knowledge of Late Woodland farming to develop intensive corn agriculture most failed to adopt other Mississippian characteristics. Hunting, fishing and foraging continued to be important but the improved agricultural techniques explain why their towns increased in size and are typically located along rivers. The historic Algonkin of the Tidewater regions and Tuscarora on the inland Coastal Plain do not appear to have constructed earthen mounds. In North Carolina's Piedmont, the palisade Town Creek site in Montgomery County is known to have a large, platform mound with a thatched roof, waddle-and-daub ceremonial building on top with other houses located nearby (See following photograph).

Elsewhere, the protohistoric Piedmont Catawba and Appalachian Summit Cherokee are considered by some to be descendants of mound builders; however, current research provides only limited evidence to suggest a true Mississippian tradition. The southwest mountains of North Carolina may eventually prove to be a different story. During the Late Woodland a local Connestee culture exhibits contact with the Ohio Mississippian Hopewell peoples. Earthen mounds are one characteristic of the Connestee, along with a Hopewell-like flint napping technology that produced arrow points from polyhedral cores of chert and chalcedony. (Chapman and Keel) Other Hopewell-like artifacts include zoomorphic or anthropomorphic clay figurines and the use of cross-hatched designs on pottery rims. Trade between the Ohio valley and western North Carolina may have initiated this Mississippian influence, since Hopewellian sites in the Ohio include artifacts of mica, quartz crystals and steatite found in western North Carolina's mountains.

Mounds are also found in the southern Appalachian Summit at Peachtree in Macon County (Setzler and Jennings) and Garden Creek along the Pigeon River in Haywood County (Dickens 1976). Also discovered in this region was a large, twenty-three feet in diameter building at a Tuckasegee site in Jackson County which may have served as a regional ceremonial center. (Keel 1976) In another example, the Warren Wilson site in Buncombe County along Swannanoa River is one of the most significant late prehistoric locations in North Carolina's southern Appalachian Summit. First occupied by Native Americans in the Middle Archaic, archaeologists have since excavated a palisade walled village that dates to a Mississippian culture named Pisgah.

In fact, Pisgah culture appears to change during the succeeding 1500s to 1800s into a Qualla Phase, the protohistoric culture of the later Cherokee. (Dickens 1976, Keel 1976) Mississippian-type earthen mounds are also found along the eastern Appalachian foothills in Burke and adjacent McDowell and Caldwell counties. Archaeologist David Moore concludes: "As far as is known, mounds in the mountain region were substructure mounds with buildings placed on their summits. They sometimes served for contemporary and/or later intrusive [burials]. It is likely that most of their use occurred during the late prehistoric and protohistoric periods." Under his direction, excavations at the Berry farm site in Burke County and historical records (Thomas, *Annual Report of American Ethnology*, 1879) indicate an earthen mound was located in the 16th century historic native town of Joara — also the site for Spain's Fort San Juan constructed in 1567.

THE OLD SACRED THINGS

When they were ready to build a mound, they lay a circle of stones on the ground. Next, they made a fire in the center and put near it the body of some prominent chief or priest together with an Ulunsu'ti stone, an uktena scale or horn, a feather from an eagle or great tla'nuwa, which lived in those days, and beads of seven colors. A priest then conjured up diseases for these things to kill anyone who would destroy the townhouse. The mound was built-up with earth brought by women in baskets. They piled earth over everything, except the fire which was protected with a hollow cedar trunk that would reach up into the townhouse. After the mound was finished, the townhouse was built on the top.
The Fire Keeper always tended the hot coals, and when there was a dance or council he would feed the coals with long stalks of ihya'ga weed and place lichen around the top. As he prayed, the fire would climb up the stalks and burn the lichen. The Fire Keeper then

placed wood on the fire for the dancers or council. Afterwards he would cover the fire with ashes -- but the coals were never put out. In the old days, all towns extinguished their fires before the Green Corn Dance and came to this townhouse to get new fire. This was called atsi'la galunkw'ti yu, or the "scared fire."(Cherokee. Adapted from Gloria Levitas et al, *American Indian Prose and Poetry*, 6.)

Town Creek Mississippian Mound

This 14th century earthen mound is located within the reconstructed site of Town Creek, a state park in the North Carolina piedmont near Mt. Gilead, Montgomery County. Enclosed with a palisade wall, the large town also includes homes and other structures, one of which includes burials. Courtesy North Carolina Department of Cultural Resources, Division of Archives and History.

Native American Food Recipes

(From Sharpe and Underwood, *American Indian Cooking & Herb Lore.*)

Fish Soup: Boil whole fish of any kind in a pot filled with water until meat is tender. Remove heads and bones. Stir cornmeal into stew until thick. Add wild onions or other greens for flavor.

Acorn Stew: Cut deer, bird, squirrel or other game meat into small bite-size pieces and cook in water until well done. Grind shelled acorns into a flour. Strain broth from the meat. Shred meat and mix in bowl with the acorn flour. Pour the broth over this mixture and stir.

Wild Game Stew: Cut game meat into chucks and boil in water until very tender. Remove bones if necessary. In a separate bowl, pour some broth into corn flour for dough. Flatten dough and cut into strips. Add dumpling strips to boiling pot of meat and broth until cooked. Add several eggs to pot, but do not stir until eggs are cooked. Serve hot.

Fried Meats: Dress game meat, slicing into large pieces. Wash meat and cover in bowl with water. Boil until tender. Remove each piece from bowl and roll in corn flour mixed with eggs. Add animal fat to flat hot rock and fry until brown.

Chestnut Bread: Peel chestnuts and crush into pieces. Mix cornmeal with chestnuts in boiling water until thick. Remove portion of mixture and place on a green corn shuck. Wrap and tie each bundle securely. Place each bundle into a pot of boiling water and simmer. Remove and unwrap bundle to eat bread. Beans may substitute for chestnuts.

Sweet Potatoes with Hickory Nut Sauce: Beat a cup of hickory nut meat into a smooth butter. Roll into small balls. Bake several sweet potatoes until well done. Peel skins and place in bowl. With the nut balls in a separate bowl, pour a small amount of hot water on each ball and stir until they dissolve. Pour nut sauce over potatoes and serve.

Bean Balls: Boil brown beans in water until tender. Place cornmeal into large mixing bowl and add hot beans with some soup until the mixture is a stiff dough. Roll into balls and drop into pot of boiling water. Cook slowly, then serve.

Corn Mush: Boil cornmeal or shelled kernel corn in pot with water until cooked. Add meat broth, nuts, beans or fruit for flavor. Simmer mixture until served.

Sassafras Tea: Scrape and clean several roots from the Sassafras bush. Place roots in small pot of water and slowly bring to a boil. Remove from heat and simmer. May add honey.

Early Colonial History: Native Americans became a part of European history as explorers arrived in the New World during the 16th century. All to quickly Spaniards conquered the Aztec in Mexico, Inca of Peru, founded *La Florida* and trekked across the Carolinas. During the following century English colonists established settlements on the Atlantic coast and French traders from Canada appeared on the Mississippi River. The arrival of these *U-Ne-Ga* (Mooney 1900, xiii), or "white people," caused no small amount of consternation among the Indians as they watched these strange people plow Mother Earth, fence the land, mine rocks and muddy the rivers and streams. While many smaller eastern tribes moved out before European settlers arrived, we do have written accounts about some of these native people from explorers, traders, surveyors, travelers and naturalists such as Soto (1541), Pardo (1567-1568), Lawson (1704), Catesby (1743), Spangenburg (1752), Timberlake (1765), Adair (1775) and Bartram (1791).

The first recorded exploration of North Carolina's Outerbanks and Tidewater region occurred during the summer of 1524 when Florentine Captain Giovanni da Verrazano, sailing under a French flag, mapped an area near the Cape Fear River. While the French attempted twice but failed to establish a permanent settlement on the Atlantic coast, it would be the Spaniards who eventually founded St. Augustine (1565) in Florida and Santa Elena (1566) at Parris Island in South Carolina. Most likely the first face-to-face inland encounter with Carolina natives happened in the Piedmont and western foothills along the Catawba River with the arrival of *conquistador* Hernando de Soto from Florida in the early 1540s and again with the army of Captain Juan Pardo coming from Santa Elena some twenty-five years later. His construction of several forts in the Carolinas and eastern Tennessee fail to establish permanent Spanish settlements in the interior of southeast North America.

As the English "discovered" North Carolina's coastal natives, they wrote their names as Chowan, Hatteras, Moratok, Pamlico, Secotan and Weapomeoc. Further inland they found the Tuscarora, Meherrin, Coree and Neuse who had occupied this land for centuries. In 1585 the first English colonists arrived in the New World at Roanoke Island, North Carolina, under the sponsorship of Walter Raleigh but soon returned home in failure. A second attempt two years later, led by John White, found the abandoned Roanoke camp and established a new colony with 117 people. Virginia Dare, the first English child born in the New World and granddaughter to White, made her appearance soon afterwards. In the following year White was forced to return to England for additional supplies; however, war with Spain prevented his return to Roanoke Island for more than two years.

Upon entering the Roanoke settlement in 1590, White found no one there and no evidence of recent habitation. The only clue to this mystery was the word "CROATAN" carved into a post, perhaps indicating the colonists had moved to the mainland to live with friendly Indians. Since White's ship captain was more interested in plundering Spanish ships along the Atlantic coast, White never had an opportunity to

30

investigate and the British crown never conducted a serious search for these missing settlers. Today, stories abound as to the whereabouts of this "lost colony" but no definitive answer is yet available. One intriguing tale among the Lumbee Indians of Robeson County (Dial and Eliades) recounts a time when their ancestors adopted white strangers into the tribe. Years later, it is reported by English colonists arriving in eastern North Carolina that they encountered "natives" with blue eyes — and some people who spoke English.

Although Spaniards introduced the Indians to firearms, metal tools, grain crops and domesticated animals such as the horse, chicken, pig and cow, it would be the English who learned from Native Americans how to survive on this wild frontier. Indian dress and hunting habits became the norm as colonists learned to depend upon native crops and skills in growing food. Illnesses were often treated with Indian remedies of witch hazel (*muscle ache*), ephedrine (*cold*), sweetgum balm (*skin rash*) and sassafras tea (*upset stomach*). Tobacco, cultivated as a scared plant for native ceremonies, was introduced into Spain in 1558 and into England by Sir Walter Raleigh in 1586. The addictive tobacco habit of sniffing and smoking spread rapidly across Europe and eventually encircled the world during the next century. (Spencer and Jennings)

At the beginning of its Colonial Period, North Carolina was populated by at least three native linguistic groups, each numbering into the tens of thousands: the Iroquoian, Siouan and Algonquian. (Kroeber, see following graphic.) The Algonquian tribes of Chowan, Hatteras, Nachapunga, Moratok, Pamlico, Secotan and Weapomeoc were people of the Tidewater region. The Carolina Piedmont was home to the Siouan speaking Cheraw, Eno, Keyauwee, Occaneechi, Saponi, Shakori, Sugaree, Sissipahaw, Tutelo, Waccamaw, Waxhaw and Woccon. It was here that the Siouan Catawba, "a people of the river bank" who called themselves the *Iyeye*, resided primarily along the Wateree-Santee-Catawba River which flowed from North Carolina's mountains southward across South Carolina. The third group, Iroquoian related Tuscarora, Meherrin and Coree, lived in the Coastal Plains but their Cherokee cousins, known to local tribes as "the cave people" and who called themselves *Ani-Yun' wiya*, lived in the mountains of North Carolina, Tennessee and northern Georgia.

The first settlers in coastal North Carolina came during the 17th century as English colonists migrated from Petersburg (VA) and later from Charles Town (SC). Soon thereafter trappers and fur traders by the hundreds made their way into the Blue Ridge Mountains of North Carolina. Their arrival greatly increased after King Charles granted in 1663 eight Lord Proprietors governorship of the Carolina Colony. This action opened the door to great personal profit if only settlers could be enticed with inexpensive land (50 cents per acre) to homestead in this frontier wilderness. In the next century, a significant number of German families came into the Piedmont from Pennsylvania along the Occoneeche Trail, or "Indian Trading Path," between Petersburg and southern Indian towns.

The immensity of this mobile, drifting mass, which sometimes brought more than 400 families with horse wagons and cattle into North Carolina in a single year...is attested by the fact that from 1732-1754, mainly as the result of Scot-Irish inundation, the population of Carolina more than doubled. (Henderson, 10-11)

As these European settlers spread across North Carolina, native populations either migrated out of the area or joined larger tribes. Competition for land and food resources also took a toll as these rapid demographic changes accelerated the spread of European diseases. With no natural resistance to these strange illnesses of smallpox, measles and typhus, an outbreak sometimes spread rapidly among the natives with deadly results. In fact, it is disease rather than war and acculturation that had the greatest negative effect on Indians as their numbers declined significantly throughout the southeast by the mid-1700s.

Due to disease, famine, legal decree or guns, the limited choices for Indians in colonial North Carolina came to be adapt, run-away or fight. Increasing frustrations on both sides ultimately led some Indian tribes to the latter outcome and the so-called period of "Indian Wars." Fighting began as early as 1663 near the mouth of Cape Fear River after colonists abducted several Indian children for "learning and the principles of the Christian religion." (Lee) Bloody attacks from both sides resulted in an uneasy stalemate and the potential for renewed conflicts in the future. Even decades later, as failed attempts by the Tuscarora to leave the region to join tribes in the north (plus political infighting among local colonists) resulted in the terrible Tuscarora Wars of 1711-1715.

Part of this tragic story begins with the surveyor John Lawson trying to interest Baron von Graffenried of New Bern in acquiring additional land — which just happened to be Tuscarora hunting grounds. Lawson's high-handed treatment of the Indians resulted in the capture of these two men and their tortured execution. Soon afterwards some 500 Tuscarora warriors attacked settlers along the Neuse and Pamlico rivers killing 130 colonists. As a result of this Indian "massacre" the two Carolinas and Virginia responded with armies comprised mostly of Indians (including Yamassee and Cheraw) interested in gaining favor with the English colonial government. Following a Tuscarora defeat, the survivors were assigned to a reservation in Hyde County which remained as a native sanctuary for almost a hundred years.

During the next decades the Yamassee, Cheraw and Creek of South Carolina were driven from their lands into Florida and points west. A now weakened Catawba Nation was one of the few tribes to survive these deadly wars by adapting to European customs and learning to trade with the colonists. In western North Carolina, the Cherokee at first refused to join the Carolina tribes in revolt against the colonists and, instead, retreated further into the mountains. Only later, after political skullduggery by French traders from Canada and then English officials in Charleston, did the Cherokee finally attack frontier settlements and, still later, join the British army against American colonists fighting for their independence. This ill conceived alliance ultimately brought disaster to the Cherokee Nation and retaliation from an independent North Carolina and infant United States of America. Today, North Carolina officially recognizes Native American survivors of the Colonial Period as an amalgamation of tribes, politically defined as the Haliwa-Saponi, Wacamaw-Siouan, Coharie, Lumbee and Cherokee.

Eastern Indian Tribes ca. 18th Century
Source: Ariene Goldberg, Medina Projections Inc.
with permission of National Anthropological Archives.

Burke County, North Carolina

The Environmental Setting: Burke County is situated in western North Carolina among the eastern slopes of the Appalachian Mountains and foothills of the Blue Ridge surrounded by Avery and Caldwell counties to the north, Catawba and Lincoln to the east, Rutherford and Cleveland to the south, and McDowell to the west. More than half of the county's total land area is in forest maintained by the U. S. Forest Service, N. C. Forest Service, State Parks Commission and Duke Energy's Crescent Resources Corp. Farming, a minor occupation in the area, is typically limited to easily accessible bottom lands for pasture, beef cattle, horses, hay and corn. Businesses and housing tend to be concentrated east to west along Interstate 40 and the Catawba River. With the Appalachian Mountains rising in the west and the South Mountains along its southern boundary, Burke County's climate is usually temperate with wet springs and mild winters.

It is this mountainous and often rugged terrain that has significant implications for the study of prehistoric Native Americans in Burke County. Comprised of slightly over 500 square miles, elevations vary from approximately 1,000 feet above sea level in most alluvial floodplains to 4,050 feet at Long Arm Mountain in the northwest, Burke's highest point. Surface soils are often composed of acidic sandy loam and red Carolina clay. At more than 3,000 feet, the bare stone bluffs of Table Rock, Hawks Bill and Shortoff mountains prominently dominate the Catawba River valley nearby. These weathered and eroded granite, igneous and sedimentary rocks are as old as any on earth. (Stuckey) On the western side of this mountain range, more than 3,000 feet below, are the swift waters of Linville River passing through Linville Gorge National Wilderness Area.

During 1977 Burton Purrington of Appalachian State University conducted archaeological reconnaissance surveys in northwest Burke County near Chestnut Mountain for the Minatome Corporation of Denver, Colorado, following their application for mineral leases to prospect uranium. These surveys and the excavation of twelve small squares in the proposed drilling area revealed only a few prehistoric artifacts of quartz flakes and fractured stones. Based upon this evidence and other research, Purrington concluded that it was highly unlikely these prehistoric peoples ever settled in this region and that hunters rarely traveled through these steep mountains. He also noted Burke County's "cultural transition position between the Carolina Piedmont and mountains, along with its rich treasury of prehistoric resources, offers excellent potential to enhance our understanding of Native Americans in this region of North Carolina."

Rivers, creeks and streams are also significant typographic features of Burke County which impact potential prehistoric sites. Thickets of rhododendron, laurel, honeysuckle and cane often cover their banks beside waters populated with native trout, mussels, turtles, bluegill and bass. The Catawba River, with its tributaries throughout the Blue Ridge and South Mountains, flows eastward across the length of Burke County, eventually turns south into Piedmont South Carolina to ultimately enter the Atlantic Ocean at Charleston some 400 mile distant. A major Burke County flood in 1916 deposited sediment and sand to a depth of several feet across most floodplains and prompted the construction of protective dams in later years to create Lake James and Lake Rhodhiss. It is very likely that the flooding of these areas covered significant prehistoric occupations. In fact, the Great Flood of 1916 revealed a significant site on John's River which was then plundered of its ancient relics by area residents. One Burke County citizen remarked to this author that "a lot of Indian pottery, beads, arrowheads, and stuff like that was uncovered by the flood. I remember some people came in buckboards to haul it out." Another local resident described seeing a "ceremonial pot for smoking tobacco with six holes around the outside." Another major flood came to Burke County in 1940 following a hurricane in the Gulf of Mexico.

Since Burke County is situated between the eastern Blue Ridge and western Piedmont, local flora and fauna are richly varied with a thick cover of popular, locust, maple, sycamore, holly, birch, chestnut, hickory, oak and pine on its high mountain tops and in the lower valleys. Most of the land is in re-growth forest, since logging and saw mills were major occupations for Burke County residents during the 19th century. The slopes and foothills of the Blue Ridge Mountains also contain many rare temperate plants, such as punktatum (also found in Japan), as well as northern species of confers, laurel and rhododendron. Over 700 of North Carolina's 3,000 plant species grow in Burke County.

Dove, quail, geese, heron and ducks are common sights today along with deer, squirrel, rabbit, fox, groundhog and bear. In 1752, Moravian traveler Bishop August Gottlieb Spangenburg recorded sightings of wolf, turkey, bison and mountain lion. The turkey and falcon have been reintroduced into the region and there are persistent reports of coyote and mountain lion returning to Burke County. Recently, several small herds of Canadian Elk were brought into the Great Smoky Mountains while conservationist consider the possibility of returning wolves to the Appalachian Mountains.

IN THE BODY OF OUR MOTHER

My young men shall never work. Men who work cannot dream and wisdom comes in dreams. You ask me to plow the ground. Shall I take a knife and tear my Mother's breast? Then when I die she will not take me to her bosom to rest. You ask me to dig for stone. Shall I dig under Her skin for bones? Then when I die I cannot enter Her body to be born again. You ask me to cut grass and make hay and sell it and be rich. But how dare I cut off my Mother's hair? It is bad law and my people cannot obey it. (Nez Perce. Adapted from Gloria Levitas et al, *American Indian Prose and Poetry*, 270.)

Major Burke County Topographic Features

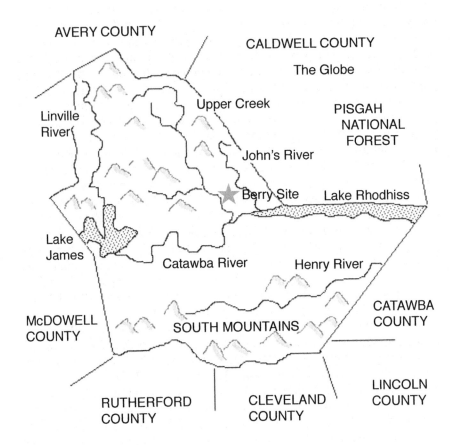

Floods and the construction of Lake James and Lake Rhodhiss during the early 20th century had a significant impact on local prehistoric and historic sites. Farming and extensive logging during the 19th century also disturbed many hill tops and much of the bottomlands in Burke County. Today housing developments and other construction along waterways and lakes are taking a further toll on potential sites.

The First People In Burke - A Brief Story

As told to me by my mother and her mother before her long, long ago, Tse-na-beka the "Bear-slayer" and leader of our ancient ancestors, stood by the rushing waters of this river, looking at the late sun hanging low over the mountains. A high, rocky peak rose to his left. Tse-na-beka felt the damp coolness of spring on his cheeks. Several wolves yipped somewhere off in the distance. Bluebird, the clans totem, sang its song. This was a good omen. Tse-na-beka turned to those following behind and asked them to set-up camp for the night. They called themselves Ka-eswa-deho, people of the river.

These dozen people of this extended family moved quickly to unpack their bundles. Two older girls, who would take mates during the next Gathering, unlashed small packs from the dogs. A pup chased a frog nearby. The girl children began to collect firewood around the camp site as the old men and boys moved into the forest to cut limbs for shelter. A young woman, Sha-meko, squatted near the river collecting rocks for the hearth, her belly, large with child, preventing her from bending over.

At the end of winter, our people left other families at the Gathering Place to the south and moved north along Big River in search of a new hunting ground. The water was now leading them westward into the foothills of the Blue Mountains, but Tse-na-beka had already discovered the paths of bison and the tree marks of elk. Many deer were seen. This river had green turtles, colorful fish and mussels. Rabbit and squirrel were plentiful. The river banks also promised grapes at summers end, and they had met no other people in three days. He felt good about these signs and this place.

Tse-na-beka remembered his childhood much further south where the summers were warmer and the tiny biting bugs were many. Over time his people became to many, food became scarce and strangers moved into the area. His family offered to travel north while others traveled in other directions. All agreed to meet each summer at the Little Mountain west of the Big River. An old woman prepared the fire.

As smoke drifted over the camp, she fanned the smoke toward her face, raised both hands toward the sky and quietly sang a chant of thanksgiving. She was Da-Jo-huppa, the healer, a person who guarded the band against evil spirits and sickness. Food appeared from gourds and bags as the group settled around the warm, crackling fire. Ba'nar, Tse-na-beka's youngest son, ignored the adults as he threw rocks the river turtles. While these people ate and talked of the day's journey, Tse-na-beka thought of the next day. This land is good, blessed by the spirits, but perhaps they will find a somewhat better camp tomorrow. If it happens, his people will call this land "home" for another season — and, perhaps, return for many seasons to come.

As a footnote to the above fictional account of the first people to arrive in Burke County, we should keep several important points in mind. Based upon present North Carolina research, it is assumed that these travelers arrived in the Catawba River Valley as early as 12,000 years ago (or 10,000 BC) near the end of the Pleistocene Epoch as the Wisconsin Ice Age began to wane. With colder climates and high mountains to the west and north, it is doubtful these Paleo-Indians came from those directions. Most likely they arrived from the south -- but could have traveled here from the Atlantic coast.

We should also understand that these first people in Burke County were fully human with the same basic needs and desires which you and I have today. Generally speaking they were intelligent, frugal and confident human beings, a self-sufficient people who survived with cunning and a profound understanding of the land on which they lived. They were nomadic, wandering from place to place with the seasons, foraging for the necessities of life. They hunted, trapped and gathered food for current consumption as well as for winter storage. The Paleo-Indian did not construct permanent structures or significantly change the environment. They packed and hauled everything of value from one site to another, leaving scant evidence of their travels or camp sites. Obviously, these Paleolithic habits present special problems for archaeologist searching for "the first" people in any location. It is thus that we create stories about their coming.

A HUNTING SONG

Comes the deer to my singing, comes the deer to my song, comes the deer to my singing. He, the blackbird, he am I, bird beloved of the wild deer, comes the deer to my singing. From the mountain, from the summit, down the trail, coming, coming now, comes the deer to my singing. Through the flower dewdrops, through the flowers, coming, coming now, comes the deer to my singing. Through the pollen, flower pollen, coming, coming now, comes the deer to my singing. Starting with his left fore-foot, stamping, turns the frightened deer, comes the deer to my singing. Quarry mine, blessed am I in the luck of the chase. Comes the deer to my singing. Comes the deer to my singing, comes the deer to my song, comes the deer to my singing. (Navajo. Adapted from Gloria Levitas et al, *American Indian Prose and Poetry*, 101.)

Paleolithic Period: Although Paleo-Indians traveled in and out of Burke County for millennia before any decided to settle in one region, only the most meager evidence of their existence is available to us today. Excavations, private artifact collections and surface surveys, however, offer important insight into these earliest visitors. Hardaway and Dalton (Clovis-type) fluted spear points have been found in Burke but all were surface finds. This leaves us wondering who left them -- transient hunters or a Paleo-Indian family actually living here? In one private collection, a local relic collector exhibited a Paleo-Indian point obtained from a farmer living along Powerhouse Road.

Professional archaeologists continue to investigate these questions in an attempt to determine the dates and cultural context for Paleo-Indians throughout western North Carolina. Most scholars believe to little is know at present to adequately reconstruct Paleo-Indian lifestyles for the mountains and foothills of western North Carolina. Robertson and Robertson reported in 1978 that most of the Paleo-Indian points found along the New River in Watauga County are made from local stone, offering the possibility that these ancient hunters either lived there or visited for extended periods of time. Earlier, Phil Perkinson in a statewide fluted point survey noted the use of local stone in the southern Appalachian region. Keel found in his studies of the Appalachian Summit and Cherokee prehistory that all the fluted points collected were south of Asheville which, according to Michalek, separates an arctic periglacial climate to the north from a milder climate to the south during the Wisconsin glaciation.

In addition to fluted projectile points, some of the stone artifacts typically associated with Paleo-Indian occupations *may have been observed* in Burke County. An archaeological survey conducted by this author examined several lamellar-like flakes in private collections characteristic of those produced when manufacturing fluted points. Associated stone chips and flakes were, perhaps, Paleo-Indian scrapers or blades along with crudely made ax heads and utilized hammer stones. Although such evidence for Burke County's first prehistoric families may be skimpy, research does support the notion that Native Americans were attracted to the most habitable locations again and again over thousands of years. Archaeologists, therefore, suspect the most heavily occupied areas in later cultural periods may contain the most ancient Paleo-Indian occupations.

Based upon this assumption, Burke County has several locations to explore — three of which have been known locally for decades. The Berry Farm (31BK22) located near the old Henderson Grist Mill along Upper Creek at Warrior Fork was exploited by relic collectors for more than a century. As recently as 1879 Cyrus Thomas reported to the Smithsonian several undisturbed Mississippian earthen mounds were on this site, along with an "Indian pond." Local legend relates that this small pond appeared as a result of Indians digging for pottery clay. In fact, a nearby resident found a small, complete cone-base, clay pot in the area, a design often classified as Archaic.

In a second example, the Michaux Farm (31BK17) located along John's River near the Caldwell County line, has also been exploited for decades, beginning in the 19th century with amateur archaeologists and dentist J. Mason Spainhour. His 1871 Smithsonian Report details the discovery of three skeletons with artifacts in a small mound "situated due east and west, in size about nine by six feet, about two hundred yards from the river." Spainhour's hobby continued for many years as he was disturbed that the Smithsonian "had a poor exhibit from North Carolina and I determined to make it equal, if not superior to that from any state." In succeeding years, with the assistance of Spainhour in Caldwell County and John T. Humphreys in Burke County, the Smithsonian assigned researchers to record these mounds and to gather new artifacts for their collections. More than once, a search by this author among Caldwell County residents, local relic hunters and museums for the reportedly "fabulous Spainhour Indian collection" produced only a comment by one person: "I saw some arrowheads on a board at a public auction in the Spainhour home some twelve years ago." It is assumed, therefore, that his "collection" now resides at the Smithsonian.

The third important Burke County example is located along the Catawba River in Morganton (31BK18). This site was damaged by past floods and the N. C. Forest Service with the 1956 construction of Edwards State Forest Tree Nursery. On this 150 acre tract a native village was uncovered by bulldozers but no attempt was made to report, record or preserve any of the Indian relics found. One of the construction workers recounted to this author how he leveled a two-foot tall "mound" in the bottoms and pushed three clay-lined "ovens" into the river to prevent someone from "stopping his work." Hundreds of projectile points and pottery fragments appeared behind plows as these workers prepared acres of planting beds for tree seedlings. As could be expected, several local relic collectors heard about this location and some even returned at night with flashlights to recover an exciting batch of artifacts, one of which included a small green stone serpent. This state nursery was recently purchased by the City of Morganton Parks and Recreation Department and converted into a public park with professionally designed baseball fields and supporting facilities. To their credit, great care was taken to preserve the subsoils on this site.

[Note: Unless stated otherwise, known archaeological sites are designated within these pages as 31 (North Carolina) and BK (Burke County) followed with a sequence number recorded at the UNC-Chapel Hill Research Laboratories of Archaeology.]

Archaic Period - the First Settlers: The forested hills and valleys of an ancient Burke County provided abundant food and natural resources for local natives of the Archaic Period between 8000-500 BC, lasting somewhat longer in the Appalachian foothills than the remainder of the state. As a highly skilled and efficient Forest-Creek-River People, there is ample evidence of their camp sites, work areas and seasonal villages throughout the region. While these Archaic hunters continued to follow large game animals, they also created ingenious ways to collect a variety of other foods. The region required snares and traps to capture small game and the invention of an *atlatl* spear thrower greatly improved hunting for deer, bear, bison and elk in thick forest undergrowth. Human sagacity also played an important part as Indians gathered roosting pigeons at night from tree limbs by torch light.

Intensive foraging by women, children and the elderly added a variety of hand-picked berries, roots and wild seeds to their menu. Nut bearing trees such as the hickory, oak and chestnut became increasingly common in the milder climates of the Holocene. In the hands of talented craftsmen tree bark, cane, grasses and animal hides became containers, clothing and housing while honeysuckle vines, wild hemp fibers and animal ligaments provided string and rope. Stone, wood and bone were manufactured into a creative assortment of tools, weapons and decorative items. Rivers and streams were the mainstay of these Archaic Indians as turtles, mussels and fish provided a reliable and constant year-round food supply. Unlike sports fishermen of today who catch fish with one line and one hook, Native Americans constructed stone traps and wooden cages in shallow rivers to catch large numbers of fresh fish as needed. Dragnet fishing was another technique used by Archaic Indians. As recounted much later by the Cherokee, the still pools of mountain streams could also be "fished" with broken branches of mountain laurel, the toxic juices paralyzing the fish that floated to the surface for easy picking. Seasonal water birds such as the duck, goose, heron and crane were captured by hand, snares and nets. Turtle and bird eggs, when in season, were easy to obtain and plentiful.

Most of the documented prehistoric habitation sites in Burke County contain artifacts from the Archaic Period. With a preference for hill-tops and areas near waterways, these materials quite often appear on the surface of weathered knolls or in lowlands subject to periodic flooding and/or deep plowing. As mentioned in the previous section, the Michaux Farm on John's River and Edwards State Forest Tree Nursery near Morganton contain multiple occupations over thousands of years which include both Early and Late Archaic artifacts. Such occupations are also common near the junction of Upper Creek and Irish Creek, about one mile west of the Berry's farm, where a nearby field contains a variety of projectile points and soapstone fragments. One private collector found a fluted point here. Further west along Irish Creek, near the State Fish Hatchery, flooding in the 1970s revealed several locations containing both Archaic and Woodland artifacts in association with heavy concentrations of stone chips and flakes. A significant Archaic site was destroyed in the 1980s with the construction of Grace Ridge near Morganton, a local retirement community situated on a hill between the Catawba River and John's River. Nearby, along the Catawba River and near the old Causby Sand Company dredge, the north bank has produced numerous stone flakes, a variety of Archaic points and a small amount of thick, red clay pottery sherds.

Additional potential Burke Archaic sites include Paddy Creek north of Lake James, Walker's Top, Steele Creek and Big Warrior Ford on Upper Creek, which may be a singular Archaic occupation since it produced an unfinished steatite *atlatl* bannerstone. Satterwhite Creek in southern Burke County also has Archaic materials, including a three-inch wide fragment of a fanned *atlatl* weight. Two knolls along Pax Hill Road exhibit large samples of both Early and Late Archaic artifacts. A local legend claims Pax Hill Road was so named because Indians "packed rocks" along a trail to mark a route to the river — but no evidence exist to prove this tale. Of some special note a Pax Hill collector found a Spanish coin in his garden dated 1790. Spanish coinage was common exchange in North America through the 18th century.

Other stone artifacts usually associated with the Archaic Period include the chipped and grooved ax, grinding stone (pestle), hammerstone, nutting stone, spokeshave, steatite pot, awl, drill and pipe. (See previous illustrations.) Such materials are usually manufactured from local igneous rock, quartz or soapstone found throughout Burke County and the region. A close examination of stone flakes at these sites occasionally reveals wear markings which indicate their use as scrapers and blades when processing animal hides or constructing wooden tools. The most commonly found Archaic artifacts, as you may guess, are spear points -- the most popular item among children and adult collectors.

Early Archaic (8000-5000 B.C.) points in western North Carolina are most often represented by the Palmer, Kirk and Stanly as identified in the Carolina Piedmont by Coe and confirmed for the Appalachian Summit by Roy Dickens, Burton Purrington and others. These point types are found throughout eastern North America as Coe speculates that the North Carolina Palmer (average 1.5 inches) is associated with an origin from the north while the larger Kirk point (almost 4 inches) originated west of the Mississippi River. The broad-shouldered Palmer and Kirk points have characteristic corner-notched stems and ground bases which may indicate an innovation from Paleo-Indian fluted points which utilized a different type of spear shaft binding. Approximately twenty-five percent of all sites reported in Clark's *Archaeological Survey of Burke County* contained Palmer, Kirk or Stanly projectile points. Two Palmer points were found in a southern Burke County apple orchard, a site known to local residents for its abundant points and, therefore, evidence of a major "Indian war" in the distant past.

Coe believed the Stanly (2.4 inches), with its typical "Christmas tree" shape, to be a continuation of the Kirk and a predecessor to later Savannah River points. It is during the Stanly phase, Coe concludes, that polished stone *atlatl* weights (or bannerstones) first appeared. Along with Palmer and Kirk points, Purrington includes the St. Albans and Le Croy types in the northern Appalachian Summit where both are typically associated with regions west of the Blue Ridge Mountains. The Le Croy, a small point with a characteristic bulge along one side, has been found on the surface in Burke County. Robert Keeler reports the Le Croy in neighboring McDowell County.

While these Early Archaic points are found in Burke County, it now seems most local stone materials are associated with Late Archaic (5000-500 BC) cultural traditions. Once again, these Burke points follow closely the sequence established by Coe for the later Archaic in the Carolina Piedmont. For example, the Morrow Mountain point with its triangular blade and tapering, rounded stem is found across western North Carolina. In fact, this point has a wide distribution over most of North America, both as a type I (1.7 inches), smaller with a short stem, and type II (2.4 inches), larger with a longer stem. The earliest *in situ* points for the southern Appalachian Summit were reported by Keel as Morrow Mountain I and II at a site near Warren Wilson College in Buncombe County. A later type, the Guilford (2-4.7 inches), has a slender, rounded, lanceolate shape and straight, rounded concave base. Its distribution is associated with the atlatl spear and appears to be limited between northern Virginia and Georgia.

The most characteristic Late Archaic point throughout southeast North America is the Savannah River, first identified for Georgia in 1931 by William Clafin. This large (up to 6 inches) triangular shaped, small stemmed point is the most abundant type found in Burke County -- and a Paddy Creek site may be a single component Savannah River occupation that also includes a thick, red grit-tempered pottery (Clark). Generally, the Clafin and Coe Savannah River types hold true for Burke County; however, some local Savannah-like "points" have a straight base (not concave as described) and, in another category, certain Burke specimens exhibit a smaller, broad stemmed point that is also unlike their type descriptions. Keel refers to such a variety in the southern Appalachian Summit as Otarre Stemmed, which he states, may be "the lineal descendant of the Savannah River stemmed point." In Virginia, Holland describes a smaller Savannah-like point as Type L. In another exception, Burke County has a broad, 2-3 inches, single shouldered Savannah-like stemmed point with either a straight or rounded small base. In conversation, Coe believed this artifact was to be a Savannah River knife blade which would be attached to a bone or wood handle.

Late Archaic Morrow Mountain, Guilford and Savannah River points have been excavated throughout North Carolina's western mountains and specifically in Transylvania County (Holden 1966:50), Jackson County (Keel 1972:65) and Watauga County (Purrington 1983:121-125). Purrington states, "Virtually anywhere one looks in the region there is a manifold increase in Morrow Mountain artifacts over recognized remains of preceding phases." These spear points are also common in Burke County. In fields on both sides of Warrior Fork (31BK13), near its entrance to the Catawba River, local residents have found an abundance of Archaic materials at "Indian Camp" and "the Council Mound." [*Once again, a local collector found a Spanish coin. This one dated 1705.*] Five miles north of the Burke County line into Caldwell County is a beautiful, lush valley known as "The Globe." Private collections also confirm the fact that this is a later Archaic location, in fact, when this author visited a local resident his graveled driveway was littered with hammer stones!

In conclusion, a few more examples of Archaic Burke County sites may be helpful. Below the hydroelectric station at Lake James along Powerhouse Road and the Catawba River, a large private collection has revealed another Late Archaic-Early Woodland site (31BK 9 & 10). A most interesting find at this location included a cache of fourteen flat, oval igneous stone blades which are unfinished projectile "preforms" or "blanks" roughed-out at an unknown stone quarry and brought here to be finished. Another Burke resident told of workers at the Lake James dam in the 1920s uncovering an "Indian grave that fell out of the side of a hill" below the spillway during its construction.

Variety in Burke Projectile Points

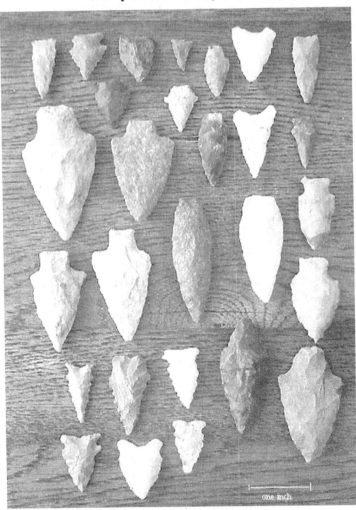

The oldest points at the bottom are represented by Hardaway, Morrow Mountain, Kirk and Stanly ca. 12,000-10,000 BC. At mid-point are Savannah River and Guilford ca. 5,000 BC followed by Woodland Period Yadkin, Pee Dee and Badin types at the top.

Woodland Farmers 500 BC - 1700 AD: While the piedmont and coastal regions changed centuries earlier from an Archaic forest efficient culture to enter a "Woodland" period, this shift did not come to the foothills and mountains of western North Carolina until about 500 BC. This transformation included enhanced food collecting methods, the hunting bow, gardening and clay pottery. Collectively, these innovations in subsistence and technology permitted relatively large, permanent towns and the development of social systems which included powerful chiefs, sizable tribes and religious centers. Much later, the Woodland cultural period becomes particularly significant since it most often defines those protohistoric tribes that came into contact with the first European explorers.

Burke County's Woodland stone artifacts are similar to those depicted for the Carolina Piedmont; however, local projectile points are typically manufactured from milky quartz, quartzite ("sugar quartz") and igneous stones. Only a small percentage are made from a smooth, fine grained quartz known as chert (mistakenly identified as "flint" by some) and jasper, an opaque colored variety of quartz found in the mountains of eastern Tennessee. Characteristic Woodland celts, polished stone discoidals (or "game stones"), drills and small projectile points have been collected at John's River, Warrior Fork, Henderson Mill and Edwards State Forest Tree Nursery. Bristol Creek (31BK1) may be a single component Woodland site.

Additional sites for this period are found along Irish Creek in northwest Burke County. One location exhibits a knoll approximately thirty feet in diameter and five feet high with evidence of both Late Archaic and Woodland artifacts in a surrounding field. One collared, punctate designed rim sherd was observed along with a flat pottery handle and a pot "foot" some three inches long. These few fragments are characteristic of Pisgah pottery identified by Dickens as proto-Cherokee. Along the Catawba River west of Morganton near Emorywood, the N. C. State Forest Service discovered another Woodland village (31BK56) when tractor-drawn drag pans revealed the upper torso fragments of a human skeleton. Two incised shell gorgets were found nearby with one clearly depicting a rattlesnake design. Elsewhere a dozen smoking pipes were observed in private collections which included tubular, clay trade pipes, one steatite and the clay fragment of a platform pipe.

Just as projectile points serve as an important diagnostic artifact of the Paleo-Indian and Archaic periods, fine-crafted decorated pottery is the most significant diagnostic artifact of the Woodland Period. Although aboriginal peoples were content to mix sand, crushed quartz or shell with clay to manufacture ceramic vessels, Native Americans along the upper Catawba River and the Yadkin River in Caldwell County appear to prefer crushed soapstone (steatite). Over half of the 58 sites reported by this author had varying amounts of pottery fragments (sherds) with this uniquely tempered clay with steatite. The brown to gray-black pottery at times had surface designs stamped with a wooden paddle. Rims were decorated with a variety of incised designs.

As early as 1903 William H. Holmes wrote that steatite tempered pottery indicated a connection to Lamar ceramics in Georgia and to the historic Catawba Indians. Based upon recent radiocarbon analysis, David Moore suggests a date of 1400-1600 AD. These steatite tempered sherds are, in fact, a unique characteristic of Burke County pottery and Robert Keeler eventually identified this ceramic type as a Burke Pottery Series based upon his examination of twenty-four local sites along with the extensive private collection of Charles and Alice Carey.

Burke Pottery Series

Paste: (1) Temper - soapstone often occurs with sand. The quantity of steatite varies from tiny particles to chunks comprising half the paste. (2) Color - exterior color varies from white-buff to dark brown and from light gray to black. No significant variation occurs from site to site. (3) Texture - paste is medium-fine and exhibits a trend toward fineness from west to east. (4) Hardness varies from 2.0-3.0.

Surface Treatment: (1) Complicated stamp comprises 61.6% of the total sample from all sites and are generally poorly made. Curvilinear designs of bull eye, spiral and filfot cross predominate. Interiors were generally smoothed and burnished. (2) Plain/burnished surfaces comprised 16.4% of the total sample from both Burke and McDowell sites. (3) Plain surfaces comprise 19.4% of the sample. (4) Minor surface treatments include check stamped, simple stamped, roughed and brushed.

Form: (1) Rims - incised decorations are used in conjunction with reed punctations or notches. Most folded rims are doubled to outside and decorated with punctations or fingernail. Plain rims are usually flattened on top and sometimes notched. (2) Body - there are apparently two major forms - the conoidal cazuela bowl and globular open-mouthed jar. (3) Base - flat, thick bottoms (0.68 cm average).

Steatite tempered pottery was also described by Carl Manson in 1948 for the Marcey Creek site on the Potomac River in Virginia. Since these potsherds were found at lower levels in association with Late Archaic soapstone vessels, Manson derived an approximate date of 2000 BC. Other archaeologists have described a similar type and a wide range of possible dates for Koens-Crispin Plain in New Jersey, Washington Steatite Tempered in Maryland and the Smyth Series in southwest Virginia along the Holston River. The Smyth Series includes net-knotted, scrapped and plain surfaces. Clifford Evans' later examination of prehistoric ceramics in Virginia found seven steatite temper sites with a total sample of only sixty sherds. He classified this type as Early Woodland and, perhaps, the transitional Archaic. In a similar Virginia study, C. G. Holland obtained a radiocarbon date for the Smyth Series of 1330 ± 120 AD. Holland also reported the highest incidence for steatite tempered pottery (35%) occurred at a depth of 6-12 inches and the "direction of movement into this area appears to have been from western North Carolina and eastern Tennessee." Howard Earnest found steatite tempered sherds along the Nolichucky and Watauga rivers in northeastern Tennessee.

Examples of Burke Series Decorated Rim Sherds

Along with others, Roy Dickens concludes that the Burke Pottery Series may be a product of the Woodland protohistoric Catawba Indians who later migrated southward along the Catawba/Santee River into present day South Carolina. David Stultz (personal communication), Curator of Education at the Schiele Museum in Gastonia, indicates only a few Gaston County sites contain low concentrations of steatite tempered pottery. The same limited results also appear to be true for Keel's southern Appalachian Summit excavations, Purrington's research in Watauga County and Fischer's surveys along the Catawba River in Mecklenberg County. Finally, one additional note. Joffre Coe's extensive studies of prehistoric cultural sequences in the Carolina Piedmont make no reference to steatite tempered pottery.

Although Keller found Burke Series Pottery at several McDowell County sites, these are statistically low concentrations when compared to Burke and Caldwell. Clark recorded sixteen Burke County sites with an incidence of steatite tempered pottery ranging from 100 percent of the sample to as low as 20 percent. Similar high concentrations of steatite tempered ceramics are also found in nearby Caldwell County. Moore concludes: "Given the predominance of Burke ceramics at [certain Caldwell] sites I suggest that these sites are linked with the coeval sites in Burke County." With examples of steatite temper rapidly diminishing from the Catawba-Yadkin locations for a radius of some fifty miles, the Burke Pottery Series may eventually prove to be a significant indigenous Woodland characteristic for the eastern Appalachian foothills — and represent the earliest pottery of protohistoric Catawba Indians.

Replicated Burke vessel based upon original fragments uncovered at the Berry site. Note the clay stamp paddle at lower right. Items displayed during the UNC-TV premier of "The First Lost Colony" at the N.C. Museum of Natural History. for The Exploring Joara Foundation. Author's photograph.

A second category of Burke ceramics, and found less frequently than the Burke Pottery Series, contains sand temper. Some research reports indicate that sand temper is a relatively recent occurrence in the Southeast and, therefore, would most likely be associated with western North Carolina's Late Woodland Period. These vessels tend to have a plain or brushed surface. One additional ceramic tradition from Burke County is a red clay, crushed quartz tempered, fabric marked vessel, less common and probably older than those described above. While more than a dozen Burke sites produce varying amounts of this pottery type, locations along Warrior Fork, Paddy Creek and Lake James in northern Burke County currently provide the best known examples.

Patricia Holden describes a similar reddish clay sherd in Transylvania County as Early Cord Marked and Early Fabric Impressed. There may also be a connection with what Clifford Evans identified as the Stony Creek Series in Virginia, although he describes this temper as "waterworn quartz particles." The Yadkin Series and older Badin Series identified by Coe (1964:30) for the Carolina Piedmont are similar to the Roanoke and Clements ceramics found along the Roanoke River in Virginia. Each of these examples is typically associated with transitional Late Archaic and Early Woodland occupations in those regions. For the southern Appalachian Summit, Keel identified a crushed quartz tempered pottery as the Swannanoa Series from approximately 20% of the sherd samples at Tuckasegee and Warren Wilson sites. This thick, red to brown pottery was often decorated by cord or fabric wrapped paddles and variously dated from 1000-500 BC. Keel further reports in *Cherokee Archaeology* that the "Swannanoa ceramics are comparable in form and style to the pottery of the Kellog focus of northern Georgia (Caldwell n.d.), the Greenville complex of Tennessee (Larson 1959), the Watts Bar focus and at least part of the Candy Creek complex of southeastern Tennessee." A summary of Keel's diagnostic description for this ceramic type follows below:

Swannanoa Pottery Series

Paste: (1) Temper - Heavily tempered with crushed quartz or coarse sand. Temper may make up to 40% of paste. (2) Color - Red, reddish brown, and light brown. (3) Texture - compact, sandy or gritty to the touch.

Surface Treatment: (1) Exterior - Entire surface malleated with cord or fabric wrapped paddle, simple or checked stamp or hand smoothed. (2) Interior - Hand smoothed but gritty.

Form: (1) Rims - Vertical or slightly incurved. (2) Body - Large to medium-sized conoidal jars and bowls. (3) Base - Conical, some with nipple-like protrusion, and slightly flattened on bowls.

Miscellaneous Burke Stone Artifacts

Depicted above at top and bottom are stone knife blades. The round object in the center is a game stone with a polished celt fragment to the left and a drilled necklace item to the right. Below these are three spokeshaves used to scratch bark from spear and arrow shafts.

Late Woodland and Mississippian Phase: After 1000 AD there appeared along the northern Mississippi River and its tributaries certain native tribes who exhibited significant cultural innovations often described as Late Woodland Mississippian or the "Age of Mound Builders." Some of these earthen mounds were built into high hills while other ground-level representations depicted giant birds, animals or humans. In Colonial America stories and myths about these ancient structures were common -- often attributed to natural events or to some vanished race of people, such as the lost tribes of Isarel -- certainly not these aboriginal "savages" of North America. Today, those Mississippian cultures throughout the midwest are known for their intensive corn agriculture, earthen burial mounds, ceremonial platform mounds and distinctive pottery designs. Their large towns, containing well constructed circular or square houses, were often fortified with a palisade wall constructed with vertical logs. Archaeologists believe that these changes signaled the appearance of dominant chiefdoms, stratified societies, extensive trade routes and complex religious customs. Only the lack of a written language prevented these sophisticated societies from being classified as "civilizations."

Eventually, the mysteries surrounding the origin of earthen mounds attracted archaeologists and ethnologists into western North Carolina in the late 19th century, especially Cyrus Thomas of the Smithsonian. Between 1879-1894, he reported to the Bureau of American Ethnology more than two dozen earthen mounds were observed in Burke and Caldwell counties. Most of these, he indicted, were low circular burial mounds. Of those few excavated, a significant number contained Late Woodland artifacts which included pottery, celts, discoidals, shell masks, incised shell gorgets and several metal objects. Thomas, who traveled extensively throughout this region, described the Berry Farm site as having one mound fifteen feet high and one conical mound seven feet high and some 320 feet in circumference. In the last century, relic hunters conducted their own "digs" and collected an impressive array of stone, bone and clay materials and, at one point, used a bulldozer to expose the largest of these earthen mounds. This action, of course, destroyed much of this potentially important archaeological feature but decades of professional excavations conducted on the Berry farm reveals that much of this sandy floodplain has preserved evidence of the 16th century Fort San Juan and the native town of Joara. Excavations continue each summer sponsored by the Exploring Joara Foundation and the Wall Center for Archeological Research.

While the extent of a possible Mississippian intrusion into North Carolina is still inadequately documented, the search for a distinctive Mississippian Phase in western North Carolina remains even more elusive. Certain Late Woodland Indian tribes in our state did develop intensive agriculture; however, only a few sites in the Piedmont and western regions are associated with earthen mounds. The historic Cherokee and Catawba are know to have had agriculture and ceremonial mounds — but did this Mississippian influence reach into Burke County?

Protohistoric Cherokee artifacts excavated in the southern Appalachian Summit exhibit direct contact with the Mississippian Hopewell tribes of the Ohio River area but, again, to what degree did their influence extend into the upper Catawba River valley? The northern Appalachian Summit of North Carolina, at present, provides no specific evidence of a Mississippian intrusion.

At this point, a strong possibility exists that Burke County's Native Americans did participate in the Mississippian transformation but much more research is required to fairly answer this question about the mound builders. In addition, since the upper Catawba River valley is strategically situated between the Appalachian Summit and Carolina Piedmont, future archaeological research must determine if Burke's Late Woodland native residents are more closely affiliated with the Virginia tribes to the north, their Siouan neighbors to the east or with those mountain tribes to the southwest.

The most current and significant archaeological studies for Burke County have been conducted by archeologist David Moore from Warren Wilson College at Swannanoa, North Carolina. Since the 1980s he and colleagues Robin Beck and Christopher Rodning have clarified and since confirmed several important issues confronting any Burke County study of the Late Woodland, protohistoric and historic periods. "Past researchers," Moore states, "have suggested that the regionally unique soapstone-tempered Burke pottery represented the material culture of protohistoric Catawba Indians. Recently, it has also been suggested that 16th century Spaniards Hernando De Soto and Juan Pardo traveled through the valley and encountered several chiefdom-level polities. Despite these intriguing hypotheses, few systematic archaeological investigations have been conducted in the region. Indeed, one could not even determine, archaeologically, if a 16th century [Indian] population occupied the Catawba valley."

With an abundance of ceramic evidence, Moore offers in *Catawba Valley Mississippian: Ceramics, Chronology, and Catawba Indians* an assessment of upper Catawba River Woodland prehistory within a regional context. From two excavations in McDowell County he observed numerous ceramic assemblages characteristic of North Carolina Woodland pottery; however, these sites also produced ceramics representative of other regions, e.g. Napier/Etowah-like pottery found in northern Georgia and the Connestee found in southwest North Carolina. The more recent Burke Series pottery, Moore believes, exhibits characteristics nearly identical to Lamar pottery from north Georgia which he tentatively identified as part of a Southern Appalachian Mississippian culture.

However, it is the Burke and Pisgah-Mississippian pottery series which Moore finds dominating the Late Woodland and protohistoric ceramic assemblages of the upper Catawba Valley. The Pisgah-Mississippian pottery, with its complicated stamped surface and elaborate rim designs, is most common along the Catawba River in McDowell County while the highest concentrations of the Burke Series tends to occur along the Catawba River in Burke County and the headwaters of the Yadkin River in Caldwell County. "The overall predominance of the Burke series is striking.... What this study makes clear is that the region features this type of pottery nearly to the exclusion of other ceramics known for the late prehistoric and early historic...Carolina Piedmont."

Moore's references to recent Burke County excavations at the Berry's farm on Upper Creek and his preliminary conclusions about this prehistoric occupation offer additional insights into the Late Woodland and Mississippian cultures of Burke County. The Berry site (31BK22) contains a large twelve acre town with remnants of more than one earthen mound. Much of the cultural evidence so far recovered are ground stone and ceramic disks, ceramic elbow pipes and triangular arrow points typically associated with Late Woodland cultures. Two excavated native burials revealed both shaft and chamber type pits characteristic of 15th to early 18th century aboriginal mortuary practices.

[Note: Laws in most states, including North Carolina General Statute 70-3, make it illegal to disturb unmarked human burials except for approved purposes. When Native American remains are identified, the grave site is reported to a local tribe. At one point in the 1990s American universities and museums housed over 30,000 burial remains of Native Americans.]

Thomas Whyte of Appalachian State University describes a Late Woodland excavation near Todd in Watauga County which contained a circular house with mud-daub roof and bark shingle walls. Most of the pottery fragments found here were crushed quartz or soapstone tempered with net-impressed designs and punctated, collared rims. The steatite tempered sherds, he suggests, are similar to the Smyth Series in western Virginia as well as the Burke Pottery Series. Radiocarbon tests produced a date of approximately 1700 AD. Based upon this and other evidence, Whyte is in disagreement with those researchers who suggest that the Pisgah-Mississippian pottery of southwest North Carolina dominated all of the Appalachian Summit. He suggests that the Late Woodland protohistoric Cherokee Qualla culture of the southern Appalachians is not found in the northwestern mountains. In another Watauga County example, Harvard Ayers found the Ward site contained a Late Woodland village with a single palisade wall and ceramics similar to those at Todd; however, these radiocarbon dates were earlier at 1406 AD and 1638 AD. Another difference occurs at the Ward site as its circular houses and related artifacts suggest a connection to the Siouan related Dan River peoples to the east who were more closely associated with the eastern tribes of Virginia and North Carolina.

How Day and Night Came to be

The animals held a meeting and No-koos-see, the Bear, presided. A question was: how to divide day and night. Some wanted the day to last all the time; others wished it all night. After much talk, Chew-thlock-chew, the chipmunk, said:"I see that Woot-Kew, the Coon, has rings on his tail divided equally, first a dark color then a light color. I think day and night ought to be divided like the rings on Woot-Kew's tail." The animals were surprised at the wisdom of Chew-thlock-chew. So, they adopted his plan and divided day and night just like the rings on Woot-Kew's tail, succeeding each other in regular order. No-koos-see the Bear, from envy, scratched the back of Chew-thlock-chew and thus caused the stripes on the back of all his descendants. (Creek. Found online at "Native Languages of the Americas," www. *native-languages.org/creek-legends.htm.*)

Early Burke Historic Period: The first Europeans known to have traveled in the vicinity of present day Burke County were Governor Hernando de Soto in 1541, who claimed this land for King Philip II of Spain, and again in the 1560s when Captain Juan Pardo from Santa Elena, the "capital" of *La Florida,* arrived seeking a land route to the silver mines of northern Mexico. In *Myths of the Cherokee* James Mooney reports several possible examples of Spaniards mining in the region, including a rock quarry and fire pit in nearby Lincoln County. The impact of Soto's passage through western North Carolina with an army of 600 men occurred without incident — but his great battle with the Creek at Mabila (Alabama) resulted in the massacre of Indians into the hundreds. Pardo's construction of forts from South Carolina into eastern Tennessee began friendly enough but lasted only eighteen months as local Indians decided to burn these forts and kill the Spaniards. Debate continues about the arrival of deadly European diseases such as smallpox and measles: surely brought to coastal regions by the Spaniards — while more deadly epidemics arrived inland decades later with English traders from Virginia and Frenchmen from Canada.

During the 17th century between 1650-1680, Virginians Abraham Wood, James Needham and other traders were instrumental in opening the "Trading Path," or Occoneechee Trail, between Petersburg near the coast and the Catawba and Cherokee towns in the Blue Ridge Mountains (Alvord and Bidgood). Several studies place one of these routes north of the upper Catawba River heading southwest into the mountains while another travels south to the Wateree River in South Carolina (Myer, Rights, Davis). Lucrative exchanges were established along this Trading Path as metal tools and cloth were bartered for Indian furs and hides. An interesting footnote to these early accounts of European travels into western North Carolina is the absence of any mention of permanent Indian villages in the upper Catawba River and Yadkin River areas.

In the following century, however, there are native villages reported to the south of Burke County (Lawson in 1704 described the "Kadapau") and west (Longe in 1714 visited the "Chariskees"). For administrative purposes, British colonial agents identified five groups of Cherokee Indians: one in north Georgia, one in eastern Tennessee and three in western North Carolina (Waselkov). An undated British archive map in Douglas Brown's *The Catawba Indian* depicts the "Cuttanbas and Esaws" on the headwaters of the Catawba River; however, the Catawba Indians are known to have moved south to the Wateree River in South Carolina by the early 1700s. While the British estimated nearly 5,000 Catawba tribal members in 1692, the 1826 U. S. Census recorded only 110. Below is an illustration of a 1720s deer skin map presented to the Carolina British governor by a local Indian chief. This map identifies fourteen nearby native towns following a road north of Charlestown, including Waterie, Charra, Suttirie, Nafaw, Cherrikies and Chickisa. Note: the Catawba, or any variation, is not mentioned.

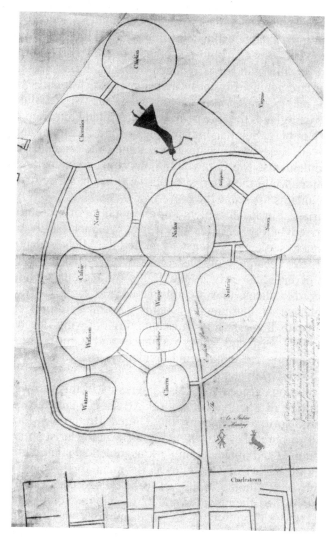

There is a persistent legend which alludes to a past war between the Cherokee and Catawba that resulted in a joint agreement to declare the land between the French Broad and Catawba rivers as a common hunting ground with no permanent settlements allowed. (Schoolcraft) The idea of an Indian treaty is given further support if one accepts a translation of the Catawba Indian phrase *eswa huppeday* as meaning "the line river" for the French Broad River in western North Carolina and South Carolina. Another present day legend in nearby Caldwell County identifies two, intertwined "peace trees" planted to commemorate the event; however, a photo of these two intertwined popular trees do not represent trees that should be more than 300 years old.

When Christopher Columbus discovered the Caribbean Islands and thereby the "New World," western North Carolina was populated primarily by two native linguistic groups: the Siouan Catawba along rivers of the western Piedmont and the Iroquoian related Cherokee in the southern Appalachian Mountains. Various estimates are given as to their number, but a reasonable estimate of this region's total native population before European contact would be something above 50,000 Indians. By 1750, however, this number is reduced dramatically after the effects of disease, warfare against European invasions, British treaties which took native lands and migration into other areas. As the two Carolinas became colonized by England, the lure of free or cheap land attracted colonist in increasing numbers. Smaller Indian tribes of the Piedmont and foothills simply moved away or, in some cases, joined the larger Cherokee and Catawba settlements. The Catawba Indians chose to cooperate with their new neighbors while the Cherokee, on the other hand, retreated further into the mountains to escape the *U-Ne-Ga*.

The earliest European settlers into the vicinity of present day Burke County arrived before 1750 as the Henry Weidner family came from Pennsylvania to settle along Henry River and the Michaux family resided along what later became known as John's River. "Quaker Meadows" was populated, perhaps, as early as the 1740s by a group of missionaries. Quaker records indicate that Meeting Houses of the Society of Friends were established in Perquimans County (North Carolina) as early as 1681. Known to favor frontier missions, in following decades Quaker settlers moved westward into Alamance and Guilford to promote Christianity among the Indians and, evidently, arrived on the frontier in Burke by the mid-18th century.

Other religious groups were also interested in this growing frontier. With the failure of a colony in Georgia, Bishop Spangenburg was sent into western North Carolina by the United Brethren (Moravians) of Switzerland to purchase 100,000 acres for a new Christian community. Their local guide and hunter, John Perkins, received a large grant of land from the English Earl of Granville as payment for his services. While John Perkins built a home in the yet to be named Catawba County, his children established their homes and farms along "John's river" in the soon to be Burke County. Due to Spangenburg's visit to the Catawba River Valley in 1752 we have the first written account of "Old Burke."

November 11: *From camp on the Catawba River... Our land lies in a region much frequented by the Catawbas, and Cherokees, especially for hunting. The Senecas [Nottoway], too, come here almost every year, especially when they are at war with the Catawbas.*

November 12: *There is not much hardwood, mostly pine.... There are many hunters here who work little, live like the Indians, shoot deer....*

November 19: *From camp on the middle river [John's River]...near Quaker Meadows, not far from Table Mountain.... It lies seven or eight miles from the Catawba but the land between here and the mouth of the river is already taken up. I think we are near the Blue Mountains....*

November 24: *From camp in the forks of [Warrior Fork?] that flows into the Catawba near Quaker Meadows. Perhaps five miles from Table Mountain.... This land is very rich, and has been much frequented by buffalo.... The wolves here give us music every morning, from six corners at once....*

November 28: *Old Indian Field, on the northeast branch [The Globe, Caldwell County?] of Middle Little River.... The Indians have certainly lived here, perhaps before the war with the white settlers in North Carolina. There are remains of an Indian Fort, grass still grows on the site of dwellings, and the trees show also that men have lived here, but it may be fifty or more years ago....* (Fries, 54-64)

Bishop Spangenburg, it seems, had second thoughts about living in the wilderness of Burke because upon reaching the Yadkin River they turned toward the east to eventually purchase land and establish Bethania near present day Winston-Salem. Others, however, would take their place on the hills and bottomlands of Burke as Joseph McDowell, an Irishman from Virginia, settled at Quaker Meadows; the Conrad Mull and Arthur Erwin families resided along Upper Creek; Waightstill Avery acquired "Swan Ponds" on the Catawba River; and John Watkins' family appear to move from place to place (Phifer). The first reasonably accurate map of Burke is most likely a 1770 sketch by resident John Collet, a native of Switzerland, based upon information provided by William Churton of Edenton, a land surveyor for the Earl of Granville. Depicted along with John's River, Warrior Fork and the Catawba River are "Quaker Meadows," "Table Mountain" and the "Montague Hills" (now know as the South Mountains).

The Indians of western North Carolina were particularly frustrated during this period by the constant arrival of European colonists into their lands. English immigrants from Georgia, South Carolina, North Carolina and Virginia continued to cross into Cherokee territory as far west as the future state of Tennessee (part of North Carolina at that time) and no number of treaties could define a protected, permanent Indian boundary. Later infections of "gold fever" and the attraction of "unclaimed land" stymied British attempts to stop further invasions onto Indian lands. Even trips to Charleston and to England by delegations of Cherokee chiefs failed to find a solution to their problem. (Mooney 1900)

During the French and Indian Wars of 1689-1763 (when England's American colonies fought both the French and Indians) the Cherokee first served with the British against France; however, before this war ended, the two allies began fighting each other. Afterwards, the Cherokee rejoined the British against the American revolt for independence — believing that the frontier colonists were lawless renegades who could only be stopped by British authorities. With this misguided belief, Cherokee warriors such as *Ata-kullakulla* attacked farms along the foothills from Georgia to Virginia. By 1775 North Carolina's General Assembly had sent troops against the Cherokee on several occasions. At one point General Griffith Rutherford reported to the state's Committee of Public Safety that Colonel McDowell was besieged on the "Catawba River and twelve persons have been killed by the Cherokee." (Ganyard) Local history also provides the story of families who fled the area when two pioneer women, Mrs. Peter Brank and Miss Lydia Burchfield, were scalped by the Indians. Mason Spainhour reports (1897) these two ladies recovered to live long and fruitful lives.

In 1730, a delegation of Cherokee chiefs were invited by British agents in America to visit London. Wined and dined, they became celebrates throughout England. Reported to have signed trade and treaty agreements which were later broken by frontier colonists. Original graphic with permission of the National Anthropological Archives.

Along Burke's western frontier, forts McDowell, White, Defiance and Charles were constructed by the British to protect settlements from Indian raids, but during the American Revolution served as staging areas for patriot campaigns against the Cherokee. During the fall of 1776, General Rutherford led a North Carolina army of some 2,400 men (with Catawba Indian guides) along the rivers Tuckasegee, Oconaluftee, Little Tennessee and Hiwasee to burn some thirty-six Indian towns and cut down corn fields. Hundreds of warriors were killed with minimal losses among North Carolina's troops. (Mooney 1900) Additional armies from Virginia, South Carolina and Georgia destroyed other Cherokee towns throughout the Blue Ridge. In May of 1777, the same year Burke County was created from a divided Rowan County, North Carolina decreed a bounty of £15 for each Cherokee prisoner of war and £10 for each Indian scalp. (Ganyard) Somewhat ironically, within decades the Cherokee became the most culturally assimilated native tribe in Colonial America, adopting English customs and, eventually, a tribal government modeled after the U. S. Constitution.

Later in that same year, treaties are signed between participating southern colonies and the Cherokee Nation to establish an "Indian Boundary" west of the Blue Ridge Mountains (Royce); however, this "Indian problem" would not be resolved until 1835 with a treaty signed by a minority group of Cherokee and the United States of America at New Echota, Georgia, capital of the Cherokee Nation. The agreement required the removal of all Cherokee in a five state area to Indian Territory in the future state of Oklahoma. This removal of the Cherokee from their traditional mountain homeland is recounted today in many native stories as the "Trail of Tears." In his book, *Trail of Tears,* John Ehle estimates that as many as 1,400 Cherokee avoided removal when married to whites as legal residents of a particular state or as a reward for helping with the "roundup" of their countrymen. Other Cherokee escaped into the mountains and refused to immigrate. As a result of these exceptions, enough Cherokee remained to claim and own property near Quallatown in western North Carolina and, eventually, become the Eastern Band of the Cherokee Nation and largest Native American tribe in North Carolina and the United States.

TRAIL OF TEARS

[An old man remembers] *Long time we travel on way to new land. People feel bad when they leave old Nation. Women cry and made sad wails. Children cry and many men cry, and all look sad like when friends die, but they say nothing and just put heads down and keep on towards west. Many days pass and people die very much.* (From John Ehle, *Trail of Tears: The Rise and Fall of the Cherokee Nation,* 358.)

Catawba Indian Corn Festival ca. 1913
Rock Hill, South Carolina

Known as a "people of the river," the Catawba chiefdom
occupied rich bottomlands of the upper Catawba/Santee
River basin centuries before European settlers arrived. For
many years the Catawba Nation was celebrated in South
Carolina during an annual festival. Photograph courtesy
of the *Rock Hill News*.

More Pieces to the Puzzle

The story of Indians in the New World is a fascinating one when you
consider for thousands of years they lived and prospered upon this land
and then, in a brief moment of history, countless tribes vanished within
two hundred years while others barely survived. Today, more than
70,000 Native Americans reside in North Carolina as Coharie, Haliwa-
Saponi, Waccamaw-Siouan, Eastern Band of the Cherokee and Lumbee.
Additional detached groups of Indians are officially recognized in the
counties of Cumberland, Guilford, Person and Mecklenburg. The
Catawba continue to reside near Rock Hill, South Carolina while the
Eastern Band of the Cherokee live in western North Carolina at Qualla
Boundary. More than 40,000 Cherokee are in Oklahoma as the Cherokee
Nation and the United Keetoowah Band. Not a single Native American is
known to currently reside in Burke County.

Only the diligence of a relatively few scholars, politicians and
private citizens — along with the perseverance of Native Americans
themselves — has allowed their heritage to survive into this century.

Much of the credit for reconstructing their lost prehistoric past is due to the diligent research of archaeologists, anthropologists, ethnologists and historians. In present day Burke County, this work exists in its infancy while much remains to be learned from further excavations and research in western North Carolina. For example, three decades of work by archaeologist David Moore and others in the upper Catawba River Valley has revealed numerous native occupations throughout the region. And now the continuing excavations at the Berry Site offers tantalizing hints that Europe's first contact with these Native Americans came during 16th century Spanish expeditions into the Blue Ridge foothills. Only recently have they uncovered the remains of Fort San Juan.

The Berry Site attracted special attention after some twenty artifacts (including olive jar sherds, nails, gunflints, a piece of melted lead and two buttons) were identified as 16th century Spanish. Although seldom found so far inland, olive jars are the most common ceramic found at Spanish colonial sites in the United States. While earlier interpretations of the Soto and Pardo routes assumed they passed along the Savannah River in Georgia northward to the French Broad River in the Carolinas (Swanton 1939), later research by Charles Hudson in *The Juan Pardo Expeditions* traces their path along the Santee and upper Catawba rivers with its headwaters in western North Carolina.

This evidence and more has led to the conclusion that the Berry site is the original Indian town of Xualla found by Hernando de Soto in 1541 and renamed Joara by Juan Pardo in 1566 with the construction of Fort San Juan. These exciting discoveries now reveal not only the first European settlement in Burke County *and North Carolina* but also stands as the earliest documented European contact with Native Americans of the interior United States — events yet to appear in grade school text books. And it is these discoveries which suggest a number of opportunities for future research in both Burke County and western North Carolina early colonial history and prehistory.

For example, the 19th century contributions of Mason Spainhour, John Humphreys and Cyrus Thomas should be investigated further. Several sites reported at that time need to be revisited and, where possible, matched to private and public collections. This author, while examining artifacts at the Smithsonian National Museum of Natural History, found several items labeled as "Morganton" or "Burke County" without any specific details as to site locations. The Office of State Archaeology in Raleigh and the Research Laboratories of Archaeology at Chapel Hill contain numerous site reports for Burke and surrounding counties that are available for serious scholarly research. In addition, information about Burke County's prehistory may be hidden in maps and manuscripts at the National Anthropological Archives in Washington compiled by Hodge, Mooney, Bushnell and other researchers.

The current renewed interest in Burke's past adds significantly to a much improved understanding of the Catawba River's earliest inhabitants and colonial European intrusions — but there is some urgency in increasing this work as urban sprawl and development consume the land. Excavations conducted in the lower Catawba area by the Schiele Museum in Gaston County has identified important Late Woodland sites along the South Fork River and Crowders Creek while archaeologists at the University of North Carolina at Charlotte saved important native artifacts through contract surveys and salvage excavations during the construction of Lake Norman. The North Carolina State Historic Preservation Office contributed to a better understanding of early Burke County history by funding an excavation at the 1812 home of Captain Charles McDowell. This state office also supported an archaeological survey of the upper Catawba floodplain in the 1980s that identified over 350 prehistoric and historic sites. Today, computers and the Internet provide a tremendous amount of information to private citizens which once was available only to professional researchers.

Additional discoveries occasionally appear in regional news media. For example, a partnership between Appalachian State University and the Biltmore Estate in Asheville attracted attention to the prehistory of this 7,000 acre tract of private land where the French Broad and Swannanoa rivers meet. Excavations of an earthen mound near Biltmore's entrance uncovered evidence of a 2,000 year old Woodland Indian village. Archaeologists now suspect that this area was a location for locally mined mica traded to Indian towns in North America's midwest and along the Gulf of Mexico.

Near Bryson City, North Carolina, is Kituhwa, purchased by the Eastern Band of the Cherokee Nation in 1996 for $3 million and perhaps the most scared and beloved land of these people. Surrounded by rolling hills, Kituhwa was the largest and most important town of the Cherokee Nation in the early 18th century when hot coals from its ceremonial fire were distributed annually to other towns throughout the nation. Initial surveys of this site and of a nearby earthen mound, indicate Kituhwa was occupied by Native Americans for almost 10,000 years. Tribal leaders are now debating its future for reconstruction.

While "discovery" is critically important to regaining the many stories of Native Americans, preservation is the key to saving these for future generations. Certain tentative steps have been taken by individuals and groups to publicize this need but much more must be done to encourage local and state governments to preserve the past. In fact, the Berry Site created so much local interest that the Carl and Linda Wall Archaeological Research Center was founded to encourage preservation and public involvement in future research throughout the region. County historical societies, museums and colleges also continue to step forward and encourage the preservation of local relics and records.

Some of these attempts have been rather creative, such as the U.S. Forest Service's Passport-In-Time designed to support volunteers and professionals in excavations at Appletree in Macon County. First visited by Paleo-Indians some 12,000 years ago, this stratified site has been occupied almost continuously up to the arrival of European settlers in the 18th century. At Appalachian State University its "Time Tunnel" consists of model prehistoric living areas constructed from natural materials by students and researchers to depict prehistoric human activities in a mountain environment.

Locally The History Museum of Burke County offers colonial and prehistoric exhibits to the public and hundreds of public school students. The Caldwell County Heritage Museum and the Catawba Science Center in nearby Hickory occasionally display examples of Native American lifestyles. Better yet, the Schiele Museum in Gaston County not only supports local archaeological field research but also maintains an exhibit of twelve native American tribes in the Carolinas — the only such display in the Southeast other than the Smithsonian in Washington, D.C. Public interest in Native Americans has, in fact, increased so much in recent decades the Smithsonian recently opened the National Museum of the American Indian.

This vigilance in preserving the past requires not only the assistance of professionals, civic groups, local governments and state agencies but the proactive concern of property owners and individual citizens. Over several decades Charles Carey, a Burke County amateur archaeologists, discovered and reported a large number of prehistoric sites to the Research Laboratories of Archaeology at Chapel Hill. The numerous Burke pottery sherds which he and his wife Alice collected became the basis for Robert Keeler's description and classification of Burke Series Pottery. While teh Berry family made a significant contribution to Burke County's prehistory by permitting excavations on their land, this effort encouraged the Exploring Joara Foundation to create a Living History Exhibit at Quaker Meadows along the Catawba River Green Way with two reconstructed native houses and a traditional garden. Future plans call for an expansion of the Living History Exhibit and the opening of a museum to display artifacts from the Berry Site and the region.

Students visit reconstructed native house at Quaker Meadows.

Role of the Professional Archaeologist

Archaeology is devoted to the scientific study of prehistoric and historic peoples, both biological and cultural, in order to reconstruct the appearance and lifestyles of the past. While primarily concerned with fieldwork, their research requires knowledge from many academic disciplines when attempting to place a particular people or object at a specific location and time period within a cultural context. In fact, archaeology depends upon a growing list of related scientific specialties, including physics (radiocarbon dating), geology (earth formations) and genetics (DNA) to answer crucial questions about "when?" and "how?"

Before publication of their findings, the archaeologist consults with others in order to broaden their understanding of a particular site. These contacts may include biologists, historians or anthropologists. Anthropology is a broad field which seeks to identify and record the customs of humans, both now and in the past. Typically, anthropology is divided into four subfields: cultural anthropology, physical anthropology, linguistics and archaeology. As you may expect, each subfield has a number of specialties which, at times, appear to overlap each other. For example, cultural anthropologists gather information about manufactured materials and social habits of both primitive and modern human communities. Physical anthropologists, on the other hand, examine the historic and prehistoric biological characteristics of humans with a focus on variations in human populations over time. Linguists study languages and their origins.

The purpose of archaeology is to recover from the depths of Mother Earth the remains of human habitation, to carefully record what is found and to preserve these findings for future research. An archaeologist must constantly be aware that excavations actually destroy the site and, therefore, great care must be taken to recover this evidence. Some writers have compared this fieldwork to tearing the pages from a book as you read it — and saving each page in its proper order! Such precise research, most often on hands and knees, may require the simplest of tools such as a shovel, trowel and brush but it is the trained eye that must see everything else, since anything, everything and nothing discovered at a site may prove to be significant. It has often been stated that one hour of productive excavation will result in five hours of laboratory work to clean, identify, catalog and label recovered specimens. Detailed site maps, artifact drawings, video and photography also support a successful excavation. Afterward, decades of study may be required to reconstruct a complete chronology and cultural history of the people who once lived in an area. If you happen to have a passion for any of the fields mentioned above, perhaps your career should include archaeology — or better yet — begin by enrolling in a professionally operated field school and get familiar with dirt.

A Role for Amateur Archaeologists

Many people find enjoyment walking through woods and fields looking for plants or animals or "Indian stuff." In fact, there are far more amateurs in these subjects than professionals — and several of the most famous archaeological and historic sites described in professional journals and textbooks were first located by amateurs or landowners. Those who collect prehistoric or historic artifacts as a serious avocation (*and share their findings*) provide a valuable service to professional archaeologists about potential sites. Surface collections and familiarity with the area are very helpful. Grave robbers and relic traders, on the other hand, continue to wreck havoc at significant ancient sites from South America to Egypt and China. An untold amount of prehistoric and historic evidence has been lost to these "pot hunters" and "head hunters" who plunder the remains of a people only for sale to the highest bidder. Such practices, everyone should realize, also encourage the production of fakes for profit, a practice which can result in false reproductions which discredit the work of serious researchers. It is for these reasons archaeologists recommend that no one should participate in the sale or purchase of antiquities outside of legitimate museums, educational institutions and public agencies.

Even as a hobby, it is important for the amateur to map and label all artifacts found and to sort these materials by location. Shoe boxes, zip-lock bags and newspaper are found in the best archaeology laboratories. This effort may require a little extra work but your time will simply make a hobby that much more rewarding. Read histories and scientific reports to gather additional information about a location's past and, especially, talk with local residents and historical societies to determine if similar sites and collections exist. At some point, the serious amateur should complete a "Preliminary Site Report" (see following page) and contact a professional archaeologist. These reports are extremely helpful when permanently filed with similar information for that region.

In lieu of a written report, it is possible to discuss your site with someone at a nearby university or public agency (e.g. State Archives and History in Asheville at 828-274-6789). Professional archaeologists may also be found on the Web at the N.C. Department of Cultural Resources or by email at archaeology@ncsl.dcr.state.nc.us. While a human burial or a petroglyph will often get someone's attention quickly, do not be disappointed if no one immediately calls you about your fantastic discovery. Their duties are most likely devoted to other projects at the time and may require a reshuffle of schedules. However, your report serves a useful, long-term purpose for on-going scholarly research and supports the state's antiquity laws and federal regulations. Major highway and public building projects are required to research these files for any evidence of historic or prehistoric occupations which may require salvage archaeology before construction. In addition, a student or intern may one day need a project which includes the site you reported.

N.C. ARCHAEOLOGICAL SITE REPORT

Preliminary Form

Date: _____ Site Name/Number: _____

Your Name: _____ Telephone _____

Address: _____

Town: _____ Zip: _____

Site Location: *[Attach map indicating major landmarks and distance.]*

County _____ Owner's Name: _____

Address: _____

Site History: _____

_____

_____

Topography & Vegetation: _____

_____

Soils: clay ___ sand ___ rock ___ flood silt ___ other ___

Describe Artifacts or attach photos: _____

_____

_____

Attachments: photographs ___ sketches ___ list of known artifacts ___

Site Registrar, Office of State Archaeology
4619 Mail Service Center
Raleigh NC 27699-4619
(919) 807-6550 or archaeology@ncdr.gov

SELECTED BIBLIOGRAPHY OF SOURCES

Adair, James. 1775. *The History of the American Indians*. Johnson Reprint, 1968. NY.

Adams, J. M. and H. Faure editors. (2002). *Global Atlas of Paleovegetation Since the Last Glacial Maximum: 18,000 C14 Years Ago*. Quaternary Environments Network Online at www.soton.ac.uk. Laboratoire de Geologie du Quaternaire, France.

Allen, R. O., C. G. Holland and R. O. Luckenbach. 1975. "Soapstone Artifacts: Tracing Prehistoric Trade Patterns in Virginia." *Science*, volume 187(4171): 57-58.

Alvord, Clarence W. and Lee Bidgood, editors. 1912. *The First Explorations of the Trans-Allegheny Region By the Virginians, 1650-1674*. Arthur H. Clark, Cleveland, Ohio.

Anderson, David G. 1989. "The Mississippian in South Carolina." *Studies in South Carolina Archaeology: Essays in Honor of Robert L. Stephenson*, edited by Albert C. Goodyear III and Glen T. Hanson. Anthropological Studies 9, 101-132. Institute of Archaeology and Anthropology, University of South Carolina, Columbia.

_____ 1990. "Paleoindian Colonization of Eastern North America: A View from the Southeastern United States." In *Early Paleoindian Economics of Eastern North America*, edited by Barry Isaac and Kenneth Tankersley, 163-216. *Research in Economic Anthropology*, Supplement 5, JAI Press, Greenwich, Conn.

Anderson, David G. and Glen T. Hanson. 1988. "Early Archaic Settlement in the Southeast United States: A Case Study from the Savannah River Valley." *American Antiquity*. 53:62-86.

Ayers, Harvard G., L. J. Loucks, and B. L. Purrington. 1980. "Excavations At the Ward Site, A Pisgah Village In Western North Carolina." Paper presented at the 37th Annual Southeastern Archaeological Conference, New Orleans, Louisiana.

Baker, C. Michael and Linda G. Hall. 1990. "The Bent Creek Archaeological Site: A Woodland Tradition Settlement within the French Broad River Basin." Manuscript on file, Baker and Hall, Weaverville, NC.

Baker, Steven G. 1972. "The Historic Catawba Peoples: Exploratory Perspectives In Ethnohistory and Archaeology." Report for Duke Power Company. Manuscript on file, Department of History, University of South Carolina, Columbia.

Bass, Quentin R. Jr. 1977. "Prehistoric settlement and subsistence patterns in the Great Smoky Mountains." Master's thesis, Department of Anthropology, University of Tennessee, Knoxville.

Bartram, William. 1791. *Travels Through North and South Carolina, Georgia, East and West Florida*, edited by Mark Van Doren. 1928. Dover Publications, New York.

Beck, Robin A. 1997a. "The Burke Phase: Late Prehistoric Settlements In the Upper Catawba River Valley, North Carolina." Unpublished Master's Thesis, Department of Anthropology, The University of Alabama, Tuscaloosa.

_____ 1997b. "From Joara to Chiaha: Spanish Exploration of the Appalachian Summit Area, 1540-1568." *Southeastern Archaeology.* 14 (1):62-89.

Blackburn, Marion P. "Spain's Appalachian Outpost." Archaeology, Volume 62 (Summer 2009) Number 4.

Blumer, Thomas J. *The Catawba Indian Nation of the Carolinas.* Arcadia Publishing, Charleston. 2004.

Boyd, Clifford. 1986. "Archaeological Investigations in the Watauga Reservoir, Carter and Johnson Counties." University of Tennessee Department of Anthropology, Report Number 44, Tennessee Valley Authority, Publications in Anthropology, Number 46.

Brown, Douglas S. 1966. *The Catawba Indians: The People of the River*, 20. University of South Carolina Press, Columbia.

Bushnell, D. I., Jr. 1919. "Indian Villages East of the Mississippi." *Bureau of American Ethnology Bulletin Number 69.* Smithsonian Institution, Washington, D.C.

_____ 1939. "The Use of Soapstone By the Indians of the Eastern United States." *Annual Report of the Smithsonian*, 471-489. Washington, D. C.

Chapman, Jefferson. 1981. "The Bacon Bend and Iddins Sites: a Late Archaic Period in the Lower Little Tennessee Valley." *Report of Investigations, Number 31*, Department of Anthropology, University of Tennessee, Knoxville.

Chapman, Jefferson and B. C. Keel. 1979. "Candy-Creek-Connestee components in eastern Tennessee and western North Carolina and their relationship with Adena-Hopewell." In *HopewellArchaeology: Chillicothe Conference*, 157-171. Edited by David S. Brose and N'omi Greber. The Kent State University Press, Ohio.

Claggett, Stephen R. 1996 revised. "North Carolina's First Colonists." Office of State Archaeology, N.C. Office of Archives & History, Department of Cultural Resources.

Clark, Larry R. 1976. "An Archaeological Survey of Burke County, North Carolina." Western Piedmont Community College Pioneer Press, Morganton, NC.

_____ 2010. *Spanish Attempts to Colonize Southeast North America: 1513-1587.* McFarland Publishers, West Jefferson, NC.

Coe, Joffre Lanning. 1964. *The Formative Cultures of the Carolina Piedmont.* Transactions of the American Philosophical Society, volume 54, August part 5:120-123. Philadelphia, Pennsylvania.

_____ 1983. "Through A Glass Darkly: An Archaeological View of North Carolina's More Distant Past." In *The Prehistory of North Carolina: An Archaeological Symposium*, 161-177. Edited by Mark A. Mathis and Jeffrey J. Crow, Office of Archives & History, Department of Cultural Resources.

_____ 1995. *Town Creek Indian Mound: A Native American Legacy.* University of North Carolina Press, Chapel Hill.

Corkran, David, editor. 1969. "Alexander Longe 1725: A Small Postscript on the Chariskees." *Southern Indian Studies.* Volume XXI. Archaeological Society of North Carolina and Research Laboratories of Archaeology, UNC-Chapel Hill.

Davis, R. P. Stephen, Jr. 2002. "The Cultural Landscape of the North Carolina Piedmont at Contact" in *The Transformation of the Southeastern Indians, 1540-1760.* Editors Robbie Ethridge and Charles Hudson. University Press of Mississippi.

_____ 1990a. "The Travels of James Needham and Gabriel Arthur Through Virginia, North Carolina, and Beyond, 1673-1674." *Southern Indian Studies.* volume. 39:31-55. Archaeological Society of North Carolina and Research Laboratories of Archaeology, UNC-Chapel Hill.

_____ 1990b. "Aboriginal Settlement Patterns in the Little Tennessee River Valley." University of Tennessee Department of Anthropology, Report of Investigations, Number 50, Tennessee Valley Authority Publications in Anthropology, Number 54.

DePratter, Chester, Charles Hudson, and Marvin Smith. 1990. "The Juan Pardo Expeditions: North From Santa Elena." *Southeastern Archaeology.* 9(2): 140-146.

Dial, Adolph and David Eliades. 1975. *The Only Land I Know: A History of the Lumbee Indians, 55.* Indian Historian Press. San Francisco, California.

Dickens, Roy S., Jr. 1967. "The Route of Rutherford's Expedition Against The North Carolina Cherokees." *Southern Indian Studies.* Volume 19:3-24. Archaeological Society of North Carolina and Research Laboratories of Archaeology, UNC-Chapel Hill.

_____ 1976. *Cherokee Prehistory: The Pisgah Phase In The Appalachian Summit Region.* The University of Tennessee Press, Knoxville.

_____ 1980. "Ceramic Diversity as an Indicator of Cultural Dynamics in the Woodland Period." *Tennessee Anthropologist* 5:34-36.

Dillehay, Tom. 2000. *The Settlement of the Americas.* Basic Books, New York.

Egloff, Brian J. 1967. "An Analysis of Ceramics from Cherokee Towns." Unpublished Master's thesis, Department of Anthropology, UNC-CH.

Ehle, John. 1988. *Trail of Tears: The Rise and Fall of the Cherokee Nation.* Anchor Books. Doubleday, New York.

Ethridge, Robbie and Charles Hudson editors. 2002. *The Transformation of the Southeastern Indians 1540-1760.* University Press of Mississippi.

Evans, Clifford. 1955. "A Ceramic Study of Virginia Archaeology." *Bureau of American Ethnology Bulletin 160:69*. Smithsonian Institution, Washington, D.C.

Farmer, Brenna. 1997. "The Prehistory of Cherokee and Clay Counties in the Appalachian Summit Region of Western North Carolina." Manuscript on file. Research Laboratories of Archaeology, UNC-Chapel Hill.

Fenn, Elizabeth and Peter Wood. 1983. *Natives and Newcomers: the Way We Lived in North Carolina Before 1770*. UNC Press, Chapel Hill.

Fenneman, N. M. 1938. *Physiography of the Eastern United States*. McGraw-Hill, NY.

Fenton, William N. and John Gulick. 1961. "The Cherokee and Iroquois." Symposium on Cherokee and Iroquorian Culture. *Bureau of American Ethnology Bulletin 180*. Smithsonian Institution, Washington, D.C.

Ferguson, Leland G. 1971. "South Appalachian Mississippian." Unpublished Ph.D. dissertation, Department of Anthropology, University of North Carolina at Chapel Hill.

Fewkes, V. J. 1944. "Catawba and Cherokee Pottery-Making." *Proceedings of the American Philosophical Society*. Volume 8, Number 2:69-124. Philadelphia, PA.

Fink, Leon. 2003. *The Maya of Morganton*. University of North Carolina Press.

Ford, James and Gordon R. Willey. 1936. "Interpretation of the Prehistory of the Eastern United States." *American Anthropologists*, Part One, Volume 43, Number 3:325-363.

Fries, Adelaide L. editor. 1968. "Bishop August Gottlieb Spangenburg Original Diary and Notes," *Records of the Moravians in North Carolina, 1752-1771*. Volume One, 28-66. Office of Archives & History, Department of Cultural Resources, Raleigh.

Ganyard, Robert L. 1968. "Threat from the West: North Carolina and the Cherokee, 1776-1771." *The North Carolina Historical Review*. Volume XLV, number 1:36-50.

Gibson, Arrell Morgan. 1980. *The American Indian: Prehistory to the Present*. Chapter One: 1-14. D. C. Heath and Company, Lexington, Massachusetts.

Goodyear, Albert C. III. 1982. "The Chronological Position of the Dalton Horizon in the Southeastern United States." *American Antiquity* 47:382-395.

Gregg, Alexander. 1867. *History of the Old Cheraws*. reprint 1905. University of South Carolina Press, Columbia.

Hally, David J. 1994. "An Overview of Lamar Culture." *Ocmulgee Archaeology 1936-1986*. edited by David J. Hally, 144-174. University of Georgia Press, Athens.

Harwood, Charles R. 1959. "An Archaic Occupation Site in North Carolina." Reprint 1973. *The First Ten Years of the Journal of Alabama Archaeological Society.* Huntsville.

Harrington, M. R. 1908. "Catawba Potters and Their Work." *American Anthropologist*, Volume 10, 3:399-407.

Henderson, Archibald. 1920. *The Conquest of the Old Southwest, 1740-1790.* The Century Company, New York.

Henry, Vernon G. 1991. "Key to the Projectile Points of the Appalachian Mountains of North Carolina." *Southern Indian Studies.* Volume 40:31-63. Archaeological Society of North Carolina and Research Laboratories of Archaeology, UNC-Chapel Hill.

Holden, Patricia Padgett. 1966. "An Archaeological Survey of Transylvania County, North Carolina." Master's Thesis on file, Department of Anthropology, University of North Carolina - Chapel Hill.

Holland, C. G. 1970. "An Archaeological Survey of Southwest Virginia." *Smithsonian Contributions to Anthropology No. 12,* 170. Smithsonian Institution Press, Washington.

Holmes, William H. 1903. "Aboriginal Pottery of the Eastern United States." *Bureau of American Ethnology Annual Report 20,* 143-144. Washington, D. C.

Hudson, Charles. 1970. *The Catawba Nation.* University of Georgia Press, Athens.

_____ 1976. *The Southeastern Indians.* University of Tennessee Press.

_____ 1990. *The Juan Pardo Expeditions.* Smithsonian Institution Press.

Hudson, Charles and Carmen Chaves Tesser. 1994. *The Forgotten Centuries: Indians and Europeans in the American South 1521-1704.* University of Georgia Press.

Idol, Bruce. 1995. "The Yadkin River Headwater Region in the Late Prehistoric Period." Paper presented 52nd Annual Southeastern Archaeological Conference, Knoxville, TN.

Joara Foundation. PO Box 296, Morganton, NC 28680. Exploring Joara.org.

Keel, Bennie C. 1972. "Woodland Phases of the Appalachian Summit Area." Doctoral Dissertation. Department of Anthropology, Washington State University, Pullman.

_____ 1976. *Cherokee Archaeology: A Study of the Appalachian Summit,* 230 The University of Tennessee Press, Knoxville.

Keel, Bennie C. and Brian J. Egloff. 1999. "Archaeological Fieldwork at Coweeta Creek in Southwestern North Carolina." Paper presented at the 56th Annual Meeting of the Southeastern Archaeological Conference, Pensacola, FL.

Keeler, Robert W. 1971. "An Archaeological Survey of the Upper Catawba River Valley." Honors Thesis. Department of Anthropology, University of North Carolina - Chapel Hill.

Kimball, Larry R., Patti J. Evans-Shumate and M. Scott Shumate. 1996. "Nelson Mound Group Archaeological Project, Caldwell County, North Carolina." Report on file, Appalachian State University Laboratories of Archaeological Science, Boone, NC.

Kneberg, Madeline. 1956. "Some Important Projectile Point Types Found in the Tennessee Area." *Tennessee Archaeologist*, Volume XII, Number 1.

Kroeber, A. L. 1963. *Cultural and Natural Areas of Native North America.* University of California Press, San Diego, California.

Larson, Lewis. 1971. "Settlement During the Mississippian Period." *Southeastern Archaeology,* number 9(2):124-139.

Lawson, John. 1704. *History of Carolina.* Edited by Frances L. Harris, 1952. Richmond.

Lee, E. Lawrence. 1963. *Indian Wars in North Carolina, 1663-1763.* Carolina Charter Tercentenary Commission, 15. Office of Archives & History, Raleigh, NC.

Levitas, Gloria, Frank R. Vivelo and Jacqueline J. Vivelo, editors. 1974. *American Indian Prose and Poetry: We Wait In Darkness.* Capricorn Books, New York.

Levy, Janet E. 1987. "Archaeological Investigations at 31GS30, Gaston County, North Carolina." Paper presented 44th Annual Southeastern Archaeological Conference, SC.

Lewis, Ernest. 1951. "The Sara (Cheraw) Indians, 1540-1768." Master's thesis. Department of Anthropology, University of North Carolina - Chapel Hill.

MacPhee, Ross. 2000. "What Killed the Mammoth?" In "Who Were the First Americans," *Scientific American*, September, 84.

Manson, Carl. 1948. "A Marcey Creek Site." *American Antiquity.* Volume 13, 3:223-227.

Mathis, Mark A. 1979. "North Carolina Statewide Archaeological Survey: An Introduction and Application to Three Highway Projects in Hertford, Wilkes, and Ashe Counties." *North Carolina Archaeological Council Publication 22*, Raleigh.

_____ 1980. "31BK56." Memorandum on file, Research Laboratories of Archaeology, University of North Carolina at Chapel Hill.

May, J. Alan. 1989. "Archaeological Excavations at the Crowders Creek Site (31GS55): A Late Woodland Farmstead in the Catawba River Valley, Gaston County, North Carolina." *Southern Indian Studies*, Volume 38:23-48. Archaeological Society of North Carolina and Research Laboratories of Archaeology, UNC-Chapel Hill.

McMannus, Jane M. 1985. "An Analysis of the Lithic Artifact Assemblage from the Forbush Creek Site, Yadkin County, North Carolina." Honors Thesis. Department of Anthropology, University of North Carolina - Chapel Hill.

Michalek, Daniel D. 1969. "Fan-like Features and Related Periglacial Phenomena of the Southern Blue Ridge." Dissertation. Department of Geology, UNC - Chapel Hill.

Milling, Chapman J. 1940. *Red Carolinians*. University of North Carolina Press.

Mooney, James. 1900. *Myths of the Cherokee*. Nineteenth Annual Report of the Bureau of American Ethnology. Reprinted 1975, 35-45. Native American Library, Smithsonian Institution, Aldine Publishing Co., Chicago, Illinois.

_____ 1975. *Historical Sketch of the Cherokee*. Aldine Publishing Company, Chicago, Illinois.

Moore, David G. and Robin A. Beck, Jr. 1994. "New Evidence of Sixteenth Century Spanish Artifacts in the Catawba River Valley, North Carolina." Paper presented 51st Annual Southeastern Archaeological Conference, Lexington, Kentucky.

Moore, David G. 1999. "Late Prehistoric and Early Historic Period Aboriginal Settlement in the Catawba Valley, North Carolina." Doctoral dissertation. Department of Anthropology, University of North Carolina - Chapel Hill.

_____ 2002. *Catawba Valley Mississippian: Ceramics, Chronology, and Catawba Indians*. The University of Alabama Press, Tuscaloosa.

Moore, David G., Robin A. Beck, Jr. and Christopher B. Rodning. 2004. "Joara and Fort San Juan: culture contact at the edge of the world." *American Antiquity*, 78, No. 299.

Muller, Jon D. 1978. "The Southeast." In *Ancient Native Americans*, edited by Jesse D. Jennings, Chapter 7. W. H. Freeman and Company, San Francisco, California.

_____ 1989. "The Southern Cult." In *The Southeastern Ceremonial Complex: Artifacts and Analysis*, edited by Patricia Galloway, 11-26. University of   Nebraska Press, Lincoln.

Myer, William E. 1928. "Indian Trails of the Southeast." *Bureau of American Ethnology 42nd Annual Report*, 726-728. Smithsonian Institution, Washington, D.C.

N. C. State Historic Preservation Office. 2000. "Archaeological & Historical Notes: Burke County." Raleigh. Online at www.arch.dcr.state.nc.us.

Nemecek, Sasha. 2000. "Who Were the First Americans?" *Scientific American*, September: 80-87.

Oliver, Billy L. 1992. "Settlements of the Pee Dee Culture." Unpublished dissertation, Department of Anthropology, University of North Carolina at Chapel Hill.

Partridge, Eric. 1966. *Origins: A Short Etymological Dictionary of Modern English*. The Macmillan Company, New York.

Perdue, Theda. 1985. *Native Carolinians: The Indians of North Carolina*. Office of Archives & History, Department of Cultural Resources, Raleigh.

Perkinson, Phil H. 1971. "North Carolina Fluted Projectile Points - Survey Report Number One." *Southern Indian Studies* 23:3-40. Archaeological Society of North Carolina and Research Laboratories of Archaeology, UNC-Chapel Hill.

_____ 1973. "North Carolina Fluted Projectile Points - Survey Report Number   Two." *Southern Indian Studies*, 23:3-60.

Phelps, David Sutton. 1983. "Archaeology of the North Carolina Coast and Coastal Plain: Problems and Hypotheses." In *The Prehistory of North Carolina: An Archaeological Symposium*, edited by Mark A. Mathis and Jeffrey J. Crow, 1-52. Office of Archives & History, Department of Cultural Resources, Raleigh.

Phifer, Jr. Edward William. 1982. *Burke: The History of a North Carolina County, 1777-1920*. Private publication, Burke County Historical Society, Morganton.

Polhemus, Richard R. (1990). "Caldwell County Field Notes." Manuscript on file, Research Laboratories of Archaeology, University of North Carolina at Chapel Hill.

Preslar, Charles J., Jr. 1954. *A History of Catawba County*. Rowan Printing Company.

Purrington, Burton L. 1977. "Archaeological Reconnaissance In the Minatome Corporation Mineral Lease." Report on file, U. S. Forest Service, Asheville, NC.

_____ 1983. "Ancient Mountaineers: An Overview of the Prehistoric Archaeology of North Carolina's Western Mountain Region." In *The Prehistory of North Carolina: An Archaeological Symposium*, 83-160. Edited by Mark A.   Mathis and Jeffrey J. Crow. Office of Archives & History, Raleigh.

Rights, Douglas L. 1932. "The Buffalo In North Carolina." *North Carolina Historical Review*, Volume IX:242-249, Raleigh.

Robertson, Linda B. and B. P. Robertson. 1978. *The New River survey: A Preliminary Report*. Publication 8, North Carolina Archaeological Council, Raleigh.

Robinson, Kenneth W. 1990. "Archaeological Survey and Deep Testing of a Corridor along the Catawba River in Morganton, Burke County, North Carolina." Report on file, Office of State Archaeology, Raleigh.

_____ 1996. "Archaeological Investigations in McDowell County, North Carolina, 1988-1990." On file, Office of State Archaeology, Raleigh.

Robinson, Kenneth W., David G. Moore and Ruth Y. Wetmore. 1996. "Advances in Understanding Woodland Chronology and Settlement in the Appalachian Summit Region of Western North Carolina." Presented Appalachian Highlands Archaeology Symposium, Albany, New York.

Rodning, Christopher B. 1999. "Landscaping Communal space at the Confluence of Coweeta Creek and the Little Tennessee River." Paper presented 56th Annual Meeting of the Southeastern Archaeological Conference, Pensacola, Florida.

Rogers, Anne F. and Jane L. Brown. 1995. "Spikebuck Town: An Eighteenth-Century Cherokee Village." Paper presented at the 52nd Annual Meeting of the Southeastern Archaeological Conference, Knoxville, Tennessee.

Royce, Charles C. 1885. *The Cherokee Nation of Indians*. Fifth Annual Report of the Bureau of American Ethnology. Reprint 1975, 22. Native American Library, Smithsonian Institution, Aldine Publishing Company, Chicago, Illinois.

Saunders, William L. editor. 1886-1890. *The Colonial Records of North Carolina*. Volume V. Historical Publications Section, Office of Archives & History, Department of Cultural Resources, Raleigh.

Schoolcraft, Henry R. 1851-1857. *History of the Indian Tribes of the United States*. Volume 4. Bureau of Indian Affairs, Philadelphia, Pennsylvania.

Scarry, John F. 1994. "The Late Prehistoric Southeast" in *The Forgotten Centuries: Indians and Europeans in the American South 1512-1704*. Editors Charles Hudson and Carmen Chaves Tesser. University of Georgia Press, Athens.

Schroedl, Gerald F. 2000. "Cherokee Ethnohistory and Archaeology from 1540-1828." In *Indians of the Greater Southeast*, edited by Gonnie G. McEwan, 204-231. University Press of Florida. Gainesville.

Sears, William H. 1952. "Ceramic Development in the South Appalachian Provenience." *American Antiquity*, Volume 18. Salt Lake City, Utah.

Setzler, Frank M. and Jesse D. Jennings. 1941. "Peachtree Mound and Village Site." *Bureau of American Ethnology*, Bulletin Number 131, Washington, D. C.

Shaffer, Lynda Norene. 2009. *Native Americans Before 1492: The Moundbuilding Centers of the Eastern Woodlands*. M. E. Sharpe, New York. 1992. Online Google Books: books.google.com/books? id=QbQ8moFuVdcC&source= gbs_ViewAPI.

Sharpe, J. Ed and Thomas B. Underwood. 1973. *American Indian Cooking & Herb Lore*. Cherokee Publications, Cherokee, North Carolina.

Smith, Marvin T. 2006. "Aboriginal Population Movements in the Early Historic Period Interior Southeast" in *Powhatan's Mantle: Indians in the Colonial Southeast*. Editors Gregory Waselkov, Peter Wood and Tom Hatley. University of Nebraska.

South, Stanley A. 1972. *Indians in North Carolina*, Historical Publictions Section,Office of Archives & History, Department of Cultural Resources, Raleigh.

Spainhour, J. Mason. 1871. "Indian Relics In Lenior County, North Carolina." *Annual Report of the Board of Regents of the Smithsonian Institution*, 404-406. Government Printing Office, Washington, D. C.

_____ 1897. "Western North Carolina Indians." Speech at Women's College, Greensboro, NC. Burke Historical Collection, Morganton-Burke Library.

_____ 1900. "Indian Antiquities of Caldwell County." *Journal of the Elisha Mitchell Scientific Society*. Volume 3. Morganton-Burke Library.

Spangenburg, August Gottlieb. Fries, (1752) Adelaide L. Fries, editor. 1968. *Records of the Moravians in North Carolina, 1752-1771*. Volume One, 64-66. Office of Archives & History, Department of Cultural Resources, Raleigh.

Speck, Frank G. 1935. "Siouan Tribes of the Carolina as Known from Catawba, Tutelo, and Documentary Sources." *American Anthropologists*, Volume 37, Part 2:201-225.

Spencer, Robert F. and Jesse D. Jennings, editors. 1965. *The Native Americans: Preshistory and Ethnology*. 73-76, 490-495. Harper & Row, New York.

Stuckey, J. L. 1965. *North Carolina: Its Geology and Mineral Resources*. Department of Conservation and Development, Raleigh.

Sullivan, Lynne P. 1986. "The Late Mississippian Village: Community and Society of the Mouse Creek Phase in Southeastern Tennessee." Doctoral dissertation, Department of Anthropology, University of Wisconsin, Milwaukee.

Swanton, John R. 1939. *Final Report of the United States DeSoto Expedition Commission*. House Document 71, 76th Congress, 1st session, Washington, D.C.

_____ 1946. "The Indians of the Southeastern United States." *Bureau of American Ethnology*, Bulletin 137, Smithsonian Institution, Washington, D.C.

Thomas, Cyrus. 1879. "North Carolina Mounds." *Annual Report of the Board of Regents of the Smithsonian Institution*, 446. Washington, D.C.

_____ 1887. "Report On Mound Explorations." *5th Annual Report: Bureau of American Ethnology*, 61-71. Smithsonian Institution, Washington, D.C.

_____ 1891. "North Carolina Mounds." *9th Annual Report: Bureau of American Ethnology*, 151. Smithsonian Institution, Washington, D.C.

_____ 1894. "North Carolina." *Bureau of American Ethnology 12th Annual Report*, 334-350. Smithsonian Institution, Washington, D.C.

Timberlake, Henry. 1756-1765. *Memoirs and Travels with the Cherokee*, edited by Samuel Cole, 1927. Johnson City, Tennessee.

U.S. National Park Service. Southeast Archaeological Center. Online: www.cr.nps.gov/seac/outline/index.htm

Ward, H. Trawick. 1977. "A Summary Report of Excavations at MC41 (McDowell County)." Manuscript on file, Research Laboratories of Archaeology, University of North Carolina, Chapel Hill.

_____ 1980. "Assessment of the Status of Bk56." Manuscript on file, Research Laboratories of Archaeology, University of North Carolina, Chapel Hill.

_____. 1983. "A Review of Archaeology In the North Carolina Piedmont: A Study of Change." In *The Prehistory of North Carolina: An Archaeological Symposium*, edited by Mark A. Mathis and Jeff J. Crow, 53-82. Archives & History, Department of Cultural Resources, Raleigh.

Ward, H. Trawick and R. P. Stephen Davis, Jr. 1989. "The Impact of Old World Diseases on the Native Inhabitants of the North Carolina Piedmont." Paper presented at the 46th Annual Meeting of the Southeastern Archaeological Conference, Tampa, Florida.

_____ 1999. *Time Before History: The Archaeology of North Carolina.* The UNC Press, Chapel Hill.

Waselkov, Gregory A. 1989. "Indian Maps of the Colonial Southeast." In *Powhatan's Mantle: Indians in the Colonial Southeast*, edited by Peter H. Wood, Gregory A. Waselkov and M. Thomas Hatley, 292-343. University of Nebraska Press, Lincoln.

Waselkov, Gregory A., Peter H. Wood and Tom Hatley editors. 2006. *Powhatan's Mantle: Indians in the Colonial Southeast.* University of Nebraska Press, Lincoln.

Wetmore, Ruth Y. 1975. *First On the Land: the North Carolina Indians.* John F. Blair Publishers, Winston-Salem, NC.

Whyte, Thomas R. 2000. "Late Woodland and Protohistoric Sites of the Appalachian Summit In Northwest North Carolina." Paper presented at the Annual Southeastern Archaeological Conference, Macon, Georgia.

Woodall, J. Ned. 1987. "Late Woodland Interaction in the Great Bend Area, Yadkin Valley, North Carolina." Paper presented at the 44th Annual Meeting of the Southeastern Archaeological Conference, Charleston, SC.

_____ 1990. *Archaeological Investigations in the Yadkin River Valley, 1984-1987.* Publication 25, North Carolina Archaeological Council, Raleigh.

Worth, John R. 1994. "Exploration and Trade in the Deep Frontier of Spanish Florida: Possible sources for 16th-Century Spanish Artifacts in Western North Carolina." Paper at the 51st Annual Southeastern Archaeological Conference, Lexington, Kentucky.

Wright, J. Leitch, Jr. 1981. *The Only Land They Knew: the Tragic Story of the American Indians in the Old South.* The Free Press, New York.

Made in the USA
Middletown, DE
14 October 2023

40560935R00050